Christianity Today

k St Jo

Continuum *Religion Today*

These useful guides aim to introduce religions through the lens of contemporary issues, illustrated throughout with examples and case studies taken from lived religion. The perfect companion for the student of religion, each guide interprets the teachings of the religion in question in a modern context and applies them to modern-day scenarios.

Available now:
Hinduism Today, Stephen Jacobs
Islam Today, Ron Geaves
Judaism Today, Dan Cohn-Sherbok

Forthcoming:
Sikhism Today, Jagbir Jhutti-Johal

Christianity Today

George D. Chryssides

continuum

Continuum International Publishing Group
The Tower Building   80 Maiden Lane
11 York Road   Suite 704
London SE1 7NX   New York NY 10038

www.continuumbooks.com

British Library Cataloging-in-Publication Data
A catalogue record for this book is available from the British Library.

ISBN: HB: 978-1-8470-6541-4
      PB: 978-1-8470-6542-1

Library of Congress Cataloging-in-Publication Data
Chryssides, George D., 1945–
  Christianity today / George D. Chryssides.
     p. cm.
  Includes bibliographical references.
  ISBN-13: 978-1-84706-541-4 (HB)
  ISBN-10: 1-84706-541-4 (HB)
  ISBN-13: 978-1-84706-542-1 (PB)
  ISBN-10: 1-84706-542-2 (PB)
  1. Christianity. I. Title.

  BR121.3.C48 2010
  230--dc22
           2009050503

Typeset by Free Range Book Design & Production Limited
Printed and bound in Great Britain by CPI Antony Rowe Ltd, Chippenham, Wiltshire

To Margaret

Contents

Preface

As part of Continuum's *Religion Today* series, *Christianity Today* seeks to provide a reader-friendly introduction to Christianity. It is aimed at undergraduates, but it should also be of interest to the wider public. Most introductions to Christianity tend to be histories of the religion or else introductions to Christian theology. This book is neither. The word 'today' in the title is crucial: it is an attempt to explore present-day issues relating to the Christian faith. This cannot be done, however, without referring to the past or to Christianity's principal teachings, but these key issues are the driving force of the content.

What follows presupposes minimal acquaintance with the Christian religion. Half a century ago, one might have expected a familiarity with Christianity that can no longer be taken for granted. As Europe and the United States increasingly become multicultural and multifaith, it can no longer be assumed that readers are nominal, let alone practising Christians. Increasingly, even students claiming 'white Caucasian' ethnicity divulge that they have seldom been inside a church building and have never attended a service of worship. As the first chapter's title implies, we therefore start off with 'the basics'.

The 'Religion Today' series seeks to highlight the international nature of the religions it covers, and this book therefore tries to cover the Christian faith as it appears in a variety of cultures and traditions worldwide. Christianity has been a multinational religion since the first century, and the ensuing (almost) two millennia have resulted in an explosion of denominations, theologies and liturgies. There are estimated to be around 34,000 different Christian denominations worldwide. Because *Christianity Today* is a short, basic introduction, it would be futile to attempt to do justice to even a fraction of that number. Even itemizing their names would be impossible in a book of this size. The best an author can do is to identify the three major traditions – Roman Catholicism, Orthodoxy, and Protestantism – and discuss how they treat the selected themes. In the case of Protestantism particularly, which is the most diverse broad Christian tradition, it has not been possible to approach anything like a comprehensive treatment, and there are inevitable omissions and broad generalizations. Even seemingly simple questions do not admit of simple answers. One might have thought, for example, that it would be possible to list plainly the books that are in the Bible. This seemingly straightforward question cannot be answered simply by itemizing a Bible's contents page. Roman Catholics accept the Apocrypha, while Protestants do not. The Orthodox accept it, but give it a different name, and different traditions have slight variations in the contents, the naming of certain books, and the order in which they are arranged. All this is before we get down to questions of authorship, dating, meaning and purpose of the writings. I have resisted the temptation constantly to write that space does not permit fuller treatment of a topic: the reader must take this as read throughout, and students are advised to seek further discussion of specific themes through the bibliography.

The book's approach is intended to be neutral. It is not designed to commend Christianity, or to promote one tradition over the others. Where there are debates within the Christian faith, the aim has been to present different aspects of a controversy, rather than to adjudicate on it. The aim is to present facts, not opinion. Neutrality is difficult, probably impossible, to attain, and inevitably the author's colours may show at times. Even the selection of topics and the space given to each is arguably a bias. The principal aim, however, is not to champion any particular position, but to promote empathetic understanding of the world's largest religious tradition. Statements in the text, therefore, do not always imply my personal endorsement: for example, in stating that Jesus drove out demons, I merely mean that this is what the Bible says, not necessarily that this is what took place. I have tried to avoid the constant insertion of qualifying words like 'supposedly' and 'purportedly', and an intelligent reader should find it obvious from the context whether I am recounting what Christians hold generally, what a particular group believes, or what is found in scripture.

Despite the aim of neutrality, *Christianity Today* focuses on mainstream Christianity, and makes only occasional passing mention of groups such as the Unitarians, the Latter-day Saints (the Mormons) and the Jehovah's Witnesses. By 'mainstream' I mean a tradition or denomination that is Trinitarian and subscribes to Christianity's historical creeds. Mainstream Christians have frequently been hostile to such groups, which they sometimes describe as 'sects' or 'cults'. My exclusion does not imply that I share such hostility, but merely that boundaries need to be drawn somewhere. In any case, new religious movements (scholars' preferred term) have become a separate field of academic interest in their own right, and in order to understand the ones that derive from Christianity, one needs a prior understanding of the Christian faith.

I have tried to be 'politically correct' throughout by using inclusive language, acknowledging that Christianity includes both women and men. However, I am afraid that some of Christianity's creeds, position statements, and even modern biblical translations are gender-biased, and one author, regrettably, persistently uses the word 'it' to refer to a child. This is no doubt a matter for regret, but authors cannot change their source material. Where a group is gender-exclusive (for example Catholic or Orthodox priests), it would of course be misleading to write in a gender-inclusive way. Some Christians believe that God should not be referred to as 'he', but since this remains the standard practice in most of Christendom, I have not sought to change the way things are. Also, a few Christians want to refer to the Old Testament as 'Hebrew scriptures', in deference to Jews. Again, I have not made any such change, since my aim is present Christianity as it is, not how present-day reformers think it should be.

Finally, there are many people who have helped to make this book possible, including former teachers, colleagues and members of Christian churches with which I have been associated – too many to itemize here. I would like to thank the production and editing staff at Continuum and Free Range Book Design, and particularly Nick Fawcett, who made many improvements to the text as copy editor. Special thanks are due to my wife Margaret, who has discussed the contents of this book on many occasions, and commented on earlier drafts. It is appropriate that this book is dedicated to her, with many thanks.

Chapter 1

The Basics

Sin and Salvation

Christianity has two key themes: sin and salvation. 'Sin' is a somewhat unpopular word, used rarely in common speech, although street preachers bearing placards stating 'The wages of sin is death' can still be seen in town centres. They may be somewhat embarrassing, even to Christians, but they highlight the part of the Christian message which is not so palatable – that there is something radically wrong with human existence. If this message is unpopular, this is nothing new, since the religion's founder-leader, Jesus of Nazareth, was put to death early in his own preaching career.

Sin is only one side of the story, however. The good news is that there is a remedy for sin. The word 'gospel' is used by Christians to refer to the Christian message as a whole as well as to the first four books of their New Testament. The message is that sinners can gain salvation – also called redemption, eternal life, the kingdom of heaven, or the kingdom of God. This good news is brought by Christianity's founder-leader, who underwent death by crucifixion, and whom Christians believe rose from the dead. His death on the cross secured humankind's redemption from sin. The connections between sin, a man's crucifixion and resurrection, and the world's redemption are not self-explanatory, however, and we shall explore these connections more fully.

The Christian story begins by explaining how sin entered the world. God created the world in six days, with humankind as the culmination of creation. Adam and Eve, the first man and woman, are placed in the Garden of Eden – a paradise on earth – with the instruction that they should have dominion over the animals and plants. There is only one restriction: they must not eat from the 'tree of the knowledge of good and evil'. A serpent speaks to Eve, questioning God's instruction, and Eve is tempted to eat the forbidden fruit, offering some to Adam. The incident is known as 'the Fall' – Adam and Eve's disobedience marked a fall from grace, and as a result God cast them out of their paradise. Being the primordial parents of humanity, their deed affected not just themselves, but all subsequent generations of humans, who inherited a condition known as 'original sin'. Part of the penalty for sin is that Adam and Eve, and the rest of humankind, will experience death, contrary to God's original intention that they should live for ever. Later tradition identified the serpent with Satan – a fallen angel – and it is believed that there was a rebellion against God by a number of angels: the 'angelic Fall'.

Not all Christians believe in talking snakes. While some take the story literally, believing that Adam and Eve were real historical characters, others hold that it is a colourful and memorable story, which serves as the vehicle for religious truth, highlighting humankind's sinful nature. Though much of the material in the Bible is undoubtedly historical, Christians are divided on how literally the biblical story should be taken. The Old Testament – the name they give to the scriptures that they share with Judaism – goes on to recount the history of the Jewish people, who continually abandon God's commandments, and whom a succession of prophets constantly calls back to repentance. According to Christian teaching, however, salvation is not possible through one's own efforts, but only through the divine initiative of sending the messiah, God's anointed one. In contrast with Jewish teaching, in which the expected messiah would be a human being, Christians teach that their messiah is none other than God himself in human form. Because humankind had sinned, humankind must pay the penalty for sin. However, because humankind is unable to pay the penalty for sin, God became a sinless being in the person of Jesus Christ, whose death was the atoning sacrifice for sin. Jesus is sometimes described as the 'second Adam', meaning that he came into the world and, unlike Adam, lived a life of perfect obedience to God, paying the penalty for human sin by dying on the cross, and offering humanity a fresh start, eternal life instead of death.

This chapter is entitled 'The Basics', and hence it would be inappropriate to go into detail about how Christian theologians have explained Christ's atoning sacrifice. Some suggest that God needed a sacrifice to satisfy his honour, while others have preferred to use metaphors about Christ's death being a 'ransom'. Despite its propensity to multiply creeds and confessions of faith, Christianity does not require its followers to subscribe to any particular theory of atonement. It is sufficient for the Christian that atonement has taken place and that men and women can receive the possibility of being 'at one' (the root meaning of 'atone') with God, and obtain eternal life. Christianity therefore steers a middle course between world-affirmation and world-renunciation, teaching that God entered the world, and that eternity crossed time. It simultaneously affirms Jesus as divine – the Son of God – and human, being fully a man. The average Christian is no high-flying theologian, and would no doubt claim not to understand fully the Incarnation (the doctrine that God assumed bodily form), relegating it to the realm of mysteries that the human mind cannot totally comprehend. A line of a well-known hymn reads, ''Tis mystery all, the immortal dies'.

The claim that God became incarnate entails that Jesus was a fully human being, who lived on this earth many centuries ago. There are few historians who deny that Jesus lived, although there is much debate about who he was. (Reference to the 'Jesus debate' will be made in a subsequent chapter.) There are non-Christian sources, such as the Jewish historian Josephus (37–c. 100 CE), that make reference to Jesus, although such sources are few and tell us nothing more than is already recounted in the four Gospels in the Christian Bible. There are several other Gospels, emanating from early Christian communities, that record sayings attributed to Jesus or recount extraordinary miracles that he is alleged to have performed. Whether these texts provide an account of Jesus that comes from an earlier date than the canonical Gospels, or whether they are fanciful embellishments on Jesus' life, remains contested among scholars. Most Christians are unfamiliar with such texts, apart from scholars and trained clergy, and tend to accept uncritically what might be called the 'rhetorical version' of Christianity. By this I mean the version that Christianity characteristically proclaims. A typical Christian sermon, for example, expounds a piece of biblical narrative, drawing implications about its relevance to the congregation and the way they are expected to live the Christian life. Only rarely do clergy subject biblical stories to scholarly critical scrutiny, and their congregations would not necessarily want them to do so.

The Christian Story

It would be impossible to be a Christian without knowing the story of Jesus, found in the four Gospels – Matthew, Mark, Luke and John – which form an important part of Christian scripture. Mary, Jesus' mother, receives a visit from the angel Gabriel, who announces that she is pregnant, and will give birth to a son. Although Mary was a virgin, she would conceive through the Holy Spirit, 'for nothing is impossible with God' (Luke 1:37). Although he is referred to as Jesus of Nazareth, the Gospel writers recount that he was born in Bethlehem, since Joseph, Mary's husband, was obliged to go there to take part in a Roman census. The importance of Jesus' birth at Bethlehem is highlighted by choirs of angels, who appear to shepherds, who in turn find Jesus lying in a manger, since the local inn had no available rooms for the holy family. Wise men (possibly astrologers) from the East visit the young child, bearing gifts of gold, frankincense and myrrh.

We are told little of Jesus' childhood. The story resumes with John the Baptist, an ascetic who was Jesus' half-cousin, preaching in the desert, and calling Jews to repentance. Jesus asks John to baptize him in the River Jordan, and John hails him as the leader of a more powerful spiritual movement. Jesus then retires to the desert, for 40 days, where the devil subjects him to various temptations. He successfully resists these, and returns to Galilee to commence his ministry. Jesus gathers 12 disciples, who accompany him throughout his ministry and are sometimes sent out to do itinerant work, assisting his proclamation that the kingdom of God has arrived.

Although Jesus' preaching spanned a variety of topics, the 'kingdom of God' is Jesus' key message. What Jesus meant by this notion is somewhat ambiguous. At times he talks as if it is a future after-death state. One of Jesus' parables is about ten young women who are awaiting the arrival of a bridegroom. Five of them are wise, and have brought sufficient oil to fuel their lamps, since the bridegroom's arrival is expected at night. The other five are foolish and unprepared, and have to go out to purchase more oil, thus missing his appearance and failing to gain admission to the wedding banquet. Jesus ends this story with the advice, 'Keep watch, because you do not know the day or the hour' (Matthew 25:13). The same chapter of Matthew's Gospel contains a description of the Last Judgement, at which humans are divided into 'sheep' and 'goats', and are assigned accordingly to eternal reward or eternal punishment. At other times Jesus seems to suggest that the kingdom of God is something that can be experienced here and now: 'the kingdom of God is within [or, among] you' (Luke 17:21).

However one understands the concept of the kingdom of God, Jesus taught the importance of sacrificing the values of the present world in order to discover the kingdom. Another of his parables concerns a merchant who discovered a valuable pearl. Having found it, he sold all his possessions in order to purchase it for himself (Matthew 13:45). A recurring theme in Jesus' teaching relates to the dangers of wealth: when a rich young ruler asks Jesus how he can gain eternal life, Jesus points out the necessity of keeping the Jewish law, but adds that he must do one further thing, namely give up all his possessions. When the ruler declines to do this, Jesus remarks, 'It is easier for a camel to go through the eye of a needle than for a rich man to enter the kingdom of God' (Matthew 19:24).

Much of Jesus' ministry was to the poor and the oppressed, and there are many accounts of Jesus associating with the outcasts of society: tax collectors, prostitutes, victims of leprosy, a Samaritan woman and a woman from Syro-Phoenicia, and other Gentiles, who were either in the pay of the Romans or who did not observe the requirements of the Jewish law. Jesus was critical of the rich, the ruling classes, the experts in the Jewish law, the Pharisees, and the Temple authorities.

Jesus taught about the spiritual life. Avoiding false piety was a favourite theme: he expressed disapproval of Pharisees who flaunted their piety by praying at street corners, pompous rabbis who revelled in being given places of honour at feasts and being greeted in the street by their formal titles, and teachers of the law who insisted on having the most prestigious seats in synagogues. Jesus did not restrain himself in the descriptions he gave of them. They were like blind people leading the blind, 'like whitewashed tombs' and venomous vipers (Matthew 23:27, 33). Instead, Jesus advocated a piety that was personal, self-effacing, and came from the heart. The prayer Jesus taught, generally called The Lord's Prayer, is well known to all Christians:

Our Father in heaven,
hallowed be your name,
your kingdom come,
your will be done
on earth as it is in heaven.
Give us today our daily bread.

Forgive us our debts,
as we also have forgiven our debtors.
And lead us not into temptation,
but deliver us from the evil one.

(Matthew 6:9–13)

Most Christian services of worship include this prayer, to which Protestant and Orthodox Christians add the doxology, 'For yours is the kingdom, the power and the glory, for ever and ever.'

Regarding the spiritual life, Jesus has much to say about the Jewish law. The Gospel writers refer to him as a rabbi, and a significant proportion of his teaching is on how the law should be interpreted. Jesus is portrayed as an opponent of the Pharisees, a body of experts on the Jewish law, who purportedly were so unduly fussy about the fine details of legal observance that they forgot about the spirit of the law. Jesus says to them, 'You strain out a gnat but swallow a camel' (Matthew 23:24). Jesus is presented as someone who has greater authority than the scribes and Pharisees, and indeed even than Moses himself. In his Sermon on the Mount – an extended discourse recounted by Matthew – he repeatedly quotes requirements of the Jewish law, adding, 'But I tell you …' For example: 'You have heard that it was said, 'Eye for eye, and tooth for tooth.' But I tell you, Do not resist an evil person. If someone strikes you on the right cheek, turn to him the other also' (Matthew 5:38–9).

The Gospels also portray Jesus as a healer and miracle worker. He drives out demons, who are rendered powerless because they recognize who Jesus is (Mark 1:34). The afflicted's physical health is often associated with spiritual well-being. On one occasion a paralysed man is lowered through a roof to obtain healing (the crowd is so large that his helpers cannot get through), and is told, 'Son, your sins are forgiven' (Mark 2:5). Such pronouncements demonstrate Jesus' authority, as well as showing an important connection between physical and spiritual health.

There are several key incidents in Jesus' life. Mention has already been made of his birth, baptism and temptations. Also of key importance is an occasion at Caesarea Philippi, when Jesus asks his disciples who people think he really is. The disciples report popular beliefs that he is John the Baptist (who had by then been beheaded at King Herod's behest), Elijah (since Jews believed that Elijah would return to herald the coming messiah), or one of the prophets. In response to Jesus' direct question, 'Who do you say that I am?', Peter responds, 'You are the Christ, the Son of the living God' (Matthew 16:16). (The word 'Christ' (*christos*) is the Greek equivalent of the Hebrew word *mashiah* (messiah).)

This event is followed closely by another incident, the Transfiguration. Jesus takes Peter, James and John – his three closest disciples – up a mountain. His clothes become dazzling white and his face shines like the sun. Suddenly, Moses and Elijah appear in front of them, and a loud voice from heaven cries, 'This is my Son ... Listen to him!' (Matthew 17:5). Moses and Elijah respectively represent the Law and the prophets. Jesus frequently uses the phrase 'the law and the prophets' to refer to Jewish scriptures, and it is Christian belief that the Old Testament points to Christ. Jesus' authority is established by the appearance of these two key figures in Jewish scripture.

The greatest importance is attached to the final week of Jesus' life, when Jesus and his disciples go to Jerusalem to celebrate the Passover. The week begins with the 'Triumphal Entry', when Jesus rides into the city on a donkey and is acclaimed by crowds waving palm branches and shouting 'Hosanna!', meaning 'Save us!' The use of palms gives the name 'Palm Sunday' to the Christian festival that commemorates the event. Jesus' use of a donkey rather than a horse indicates humility, as well as the fact that he comes in peace. The shouting of 'Hosanna!' may indicate that the crowd regarded him as their messianic saviour. The crowd's acclamation is short-lived, however, for within a week Jesus had been arrested, convicted and crucified.

The Gospels record Jesus' last meal with his disciples (commonly referred to as 'The Last Supper'). It is not clear whether this is a Passover meal, but Jesus shares bread and wine, declaring that these represent his body and blood and that his disciples should continue to perform this rite in his memory. The story continues with Jesus leading his disciples to the nearby Garden of Gethsemane, where Judas Iscariot (one of the 12 disciples, who is the traitor) has arranged with the authorities to have Jesus arrested. Jesus is brought to trial, first before the High Priest and then before Pontius Pilate, the Roman Governor, who yields to the crowd's demand that Jesus should be crucified.

Jesus' death does not mark the end of the Christian story. Three days later, his tomb is found to be empty: Jesus has risen from the dead. He is first seen by some women followers, then by his disciples on several occasions. Jesus is with them for a further 40 days, after which he ascends back into heaven, returning to God the Father. Mention should be made of one further significant event. Fifty days later, the disciples are sitting in the upper room, in which Jesus had celebrated the Last Supper. The Holy Spirit descends upon them, with the sound of a strong wind, and placing fiery tongues on their heads. This event is taken to mark the beginning of the Church. (The Holy Spirit is God's active power in the world and in the lives of believers, and is regarded as a 'person', the third member of the Trinity.) The disciples become empowered, and preach openly the message that Jesus is the messiah. The event is commemorated in the churches as the festival of Pentecost – so called because the event coincided with the Jewish festival of that name.

That, in essence, is the Christian story. Most Christians know it, and probably most Christians believe that it took place in that way. It is certainly the story that is proclaimed from the Church's pulpits and in its mission. Whether events literally took place in this fashion is a matter to be considered in the chapter on modern biblical interpretation (Chapter 4). Most Christians would probably agree, if asked, that the Christian faith is not merely a matter of believing in certain historical events that happened centuries ago in a different part of the world. The importance of the Christian story lies in the belief in the risen Christ, who can be encountered in the present time by all believers. Eternity crosses time, and for the believer Jesus Christ is more than a historical figure, but a living person, sometimes referred to by theologians as the 'cosmic Christ', the Christ of faith; one who empowers the life of Christians today, through the Holy Spirit's power.

The Church

The Christian Church has three major traditions: Roman Catholicism, Eastern Orthodoxy, and Protestantism. All three traditions celebrate Christianity's major festivals. Most of the Eastern Orthodox churches use the older Julian calendar, which causes Christmas Day to fall on 7 January, rather than 25 December. The Eastern churches' liturgical year begins on 1 September, which they regard as the beginning of the Jewish year, as well as the day on which Jesus' ministry began, when he read the book of Isaiah in the Nazareth synagogue (Luke 4:14–21). The Eastern calendar alternates between feasts and fasts, while following the key festivals that it shares with the West. The Christian year in the West begins with Advent, which spans the four Sundays leading up to Christmas. After Christmas comes Epiphany, which commemorates the visit of the Magi. Lent is the six-week period leading up to Easter, the high point of the Christian calendar, being the celebration of Christ's resurrection. Unlike Christmas, the date of Easter varies from year to year, the calculations being based on the relationship between the spring equinox and the phases of moon. These factors, combined with the calendrical differences between the Eastern and Western churches, usually, but not always, cause Orthodox Easter to fall at least a week later than Easter Sunday in the Catholic and Protestant traditions. Pentecost (sometimes called Whitsun) falls on the seventh Sunday after Easter, and the following Sunday is Trinity Sunday, marking the fullness of the Godhead, who has appeared as Father, Son and Holy Spirit. In addition, the Catholic and Orthodox churches celebrate saints' days, and the festival of All Saints, which falls in early November in the West. The Protestant tradition does not favour the veneration of saints and, in the main, saints' days tend to pass unnoticed.

It is difficult to explain the differences between the three traditions in a non-partisan way, since each of them lays claim to being the true authentic version of the Christian faith. The Roman Catholic Church maintains that it is the one true Church, claiming a line of an apostolic succession that can be traced back to Jesus' principal disciple Peter, to whom Jesus said: 'On this rock I will build my church, and the gates of Hades will not overcome it. I will give you the keys of the kingdom of heaven …' (Matthew 16:18–19).

According to tradition, Peter reached Rome, where he lived and died as a result of Nero's persecution of the Christians. At Rome, he led the early Christian community, wrote his two epistles, and instructed John Mark, the author of Mark's Gospel. Before his death, Peter ordained a successor, who initiated a line of bishops of Rome. The bishopric of Rome has always been regarded as authoritative, and the Bishop of Rome became known as the Pope (which literally means 'Father'), whom Catholics regard as the Head of the Church.

Rivalry grew up, however, between Eastern and Western Christianity. The Eastern Christians noted that the West had made an alteration to the Nicene Creed. The original text of the creed stated, 'We believe in the Holy Spirit, the Lord and giver of life, who proceeds from the Father.' To this the Western churches had added 'and the Son' (*filioque* in Latin, the language in which the creed was recited in the West). To those outside the Orthodox tradition, the *filioque* dispute may seem trivial. Why should the presence of a single word in a creed be an issue which gave rise to the Great Schism of 1054? According to Orthodox theologians, however, it is important that there should be 'a single fount of Godhead', with each member of the Trinity emanating from God the Father. Perhaps more importantly, the Orthodox Church took exception to any attempt, whether trivial or substantial, to interfere with the ancient creed, since it had been agreed by ecumenical councils, representing the whole Church.

Protestantism arose substantially in the sixteenth century, and is generally traced to the work of the Reformer Martin Luther (1483–1546). Luther was a monk as well as a university teacher, and was concerned about a number of practices within the Roman Church. His opposition was sparked off by the presence of Johann Tetzel (1465–1519), a seller of indulgences, who had come to his home town of Wittenberg. Indulgences were divine favours that one could buy, which purportedly accelerated the passage of the nominee through purgatory. Luther had studied the Bible closely, and was particularly impressed by Paul's letter to the Romans, in which Paul affirmed that one could be saved 'by faith alone', not through one's own efforts. The Protestant Reformers emphasized the need for the Bible to be read, and for it to be available in the language of the people, rather than to be read in church in Latin.

It was also customary for the laity only to receive the host (the communion wafer) at the Mass, and not the cup. The Protestant Reformers taught the importance of receiving communion 'in both kinds'. They also took exception to the Roman Catholic doctrine of transubstantiation – the notion that the sacramental bread and wine literally (although, obviously, not physically) become the body and blood of Christ. According to Roman Catholic teaching, the Mass is a sacrifice in which Christ is offered up again to the Father by the priest's act of elevating the host. Protestants, relying on biblical teaching, as they do, note that scripture speaks of Christ's sacrifice on the cross being 'once for all', and hence unrepeatable. Additionally, Protestants held that the believer could gain direct access to God. He or she did not need a priest to pronounce the forgiveness of one's sin, or saints to act as intermediaries, but could approach God directly. 'The priesthood of all believers' is an expression characteristically associated with Luther, but it should not be misunderstood. Most Protestant denominations have clergy, rather than lay leadership, but avoid using the word 'priest' to describe them, preferring terms like 'minister' or 'pastor'.

The Roman Catholic Church is a single worldwide Church, centred in Rome, with centralized authority. The Orthodox Churches are a kind of federation of national Churches, each autocephalous (with its own head): thus, there is the Greek Orthodox, the Russian Orthodox, the Serbian Orthodox and so on. Protestantism grew up in a variety of European countries – mainly Switzerland, the Netherlands, Germany and Britain – with various Protestant Reformers teaching somewhat different doctrines, and often disagreeing acrimoniously with each other. The differences between Catholic and Protestant worship were more pronounced before the Second Vatican Council, which was convened by Pope John XXIII and met during the period 1962–5. Until then, the Catholic Mass was in Latin, and the laity received only the host. Orthodoxy and Catholicism offer the sacrament of Holy Communion at their principal Sunday services, which they respectively call the Divine Liturgy and the Mass, and follow a 'fixed liturgy' – that is to say, the service is a formal one, with predetermined content, in which the only scope for creativity rests in the priest's sermon.

Protestant churches tend to be simpler in design. This is partly due to the Reformers' desire to discourage the veneration of saints and of the Virgin Mary, and partly due to their objections to the massive expense that is involved in elaborate buildings. Clergy wear simpler robes, and in some traditions, such as Pentecostalism, where pastors are not formally trained but appointed from within their congregations, smart ordinary clothes are the norm. Pentecostalism is usually traced back to a revivalist meeting in Azusa Street, Los Angeles, held in 1906, where members started to pray ecstatically, making utterances that were not recognizable as any human language. They believe that this phenomenon (*glossolalia* – speaking in tongues) was what the early disciples experienced when the Holy Spirit descended at the first Pentecost (Acts 2:4). Spontaneous contributions from members at Pentecostalist worship is therefore encouraged, rather than the following of a formal traditional liturgy.

Anglicans

Mention should be made of the Anglican tradition, which does not fit readily into this threefold division of Christian traditions. Anglicanism originated in the Church in England, in which King Henry VIII assumed the place of the Pope as 'supreme governor' of the English Church. Ever since that time, the monarch has been the Church's titular head, and the Church of England the 'established religion' in the country. In practice, in the twenty-first century the monarch has little role to play in the Church's decision-making, although the civic role of the Church of England remains. Occasions like royal weddings and funerals use the Church of England rather than any other denomination, and Britain's kings and queens must be Anglicans. Some of the Church's bishops have a political role as members of the House of Lords. The changes that the Protestant Reformation brought about in England were not as great as those elsewhere in Europe, and whether the Church of England is truly Protestant is a debatable point. It is often described as 'catholic and reformed' – a compromise position. The term 'Anglican' is wider than 'Church of England', and refers to the tradition worldwide. Anglicans – also called Episcopalians – share the same beliefs and style of worship as their partners in England, are 'in full communion' with the Church of England, and acknowledge the Archbishop of Canterbury as their leader.

All three major traditions regard weekly congregational worship as an expression of commitment. Sunday is designated as the appropriate day of worship, being the day on which Christ rose from the dead. A small proportion of Protestants, such as the Seventh-day Adventists, prefer to worship on a Saturday, believing that the Bible designates the Jewish sabbath as the day of rest and devotion. In all traditions, congregational worship consists of prayers, readings from the Bible, and usually hymns and a sermon. Music is an important part of most services. Many churches have their own – sometimes professional – choirs to lead the singing, and in the Protestant and Catholic traditions the organ is the most favoured instrument to accompany the congregation. Some congregations now prefer to use a band or pop group instead of the more staid organ accompaniment. In Orthodoxy, singing is unaccompanied, and tends to be performed exclusively by a choir, rather than involving the congregation.

In Protestant churches the style of service is somewhat less formal than that of Catholicism and Orthodoxy. Although many denominations have published official service books over the years, these are merely for the officiant's guidance, and are generally disregarded. Usually there are local conventions regarding the order that the service follows, and it would certainly contain the key ingredients of prayer, Bible reading, hymns and preaching. There is more scope for lay involvement in worship in the Protestant tradition, although Catholicism and Anglicanism now encourage lay members to read lessons and lead some of the prayers.

Lifestyle

All religions offer guidance for life, and Christianity is no exception. Mention was made earlier of the somewhat ambivalent attitude that Christianity displays to the world, which is originally good, but fallen. Because God's creation is good, Christians do not regard withdrawal from the world as necessary to obtain salvation, although it is true that Christianity has had its share of hermits and recluses, and continues to have monastic orders within the Catholic, Orthodox and (to a lesser extent) Anglican traditions. Monasticism tends to be disapproved of in Protestant circles, which are much more inclined to favour entering into the world of work and family life. A few Protestant traditions have separated themselves away from the world by forming their own distinctive communities. Probably the best known of these are the Amish, who decline to use modern technology, but have traditionally enjoyed a modest lifestyle, predominantly based on agriculture.

In John's Gospel, Jesus is reported as saying that his followers are 'in the world' but 'not of the world' (John 17:13–19). Christians do not typically feel obliged to wear religious symbols, unlike the Jewish Hasidim who are recognizable by their black clothes and prayer caps, or Khalsa Sikhs who are identified by their turbans. Some Christians may elect to wear a necklace with a cross or crucifix, and the use of the fish symbol as a lapel badge or a car bumper sticker has grown in popularity in recent times. (The fish is an ancient Christian symbol. The Greek word *ichthus*, meaning 'fish', is an acronym for 'Jesus Christ, Son of God, Saviour'.) Christians who display their religious identity in such ways, however, do so from choice, rather than obligation. Apart from the Church's clergy, most of whom wear recognizable attire, such as a clerical collar, most Christians are visually indistinguishable from those who do not belong to the Church. The same is true regarding diet. Although a minority of Christians, particularly in the Adventist tradition, feel obliged to observe the Jewish food laws, Christians more usually hold that they are now free from the Jewish law. There are some Christian vegetarians, again a minority, but any decision not to eat meat is a personal one. Jesus himself certainly was not a vegetarian: he reportedly ate fish, and at least four of his disciples were fishermen.

For Christians, the key rule of life is to love one's neighbour as oneself. When Jesus is asked 'Which is the greatest commandment in the Law?' he replies, 'Love the Lord your God with all your heart and with all your soul and with all your mind ... and ... Love your neighbour as yourself' (see Matthew 22:35–40). This 'golden rule' or 'ethic of reciprocity' is by no means exclusive to Christianity, and close parallels can be found in every major world religion, as well as in secular ethical writings. Jesus claimed no uniqueness for this teaching, which he acknowledged as the central part of the Jewish law. Christianity teaches the cultivation of virtues, which Paul lists as 'love, joy, peace, patience, kindness, goodness, faithfulness, gentleness and self-control' (Galatians 5:22–3). Christians are expected to be caring in their relationships with other people, to be ready to perform acts of kindness and hospitality, to be honest in their dealings, to be forgiving, to show humility, and to restrain negative emotions and desires such as lust, anger, resentment, greed and jealousy.

There is nothing here that other religions or secular humanism would not endorse. Christians aim not to be distinctive, but to have integrity. Marriage partners who are unfaithful to their spouses, workers who fiddle their tax returns, and priests (or laity) who molest children act contrary to their faith. This is not to say that Christians never do any of these things. Although Jesus commanded his followers to 'Be perfect ... as your heavenly Father is perfect' (Matthew 5:48), most, if not all, Christians fall short of this standard since, as Paul said, 'all have sinned and fall short of the glory of God' (Romans 3:23). Religions hold up ideals to aspire to, and Christians frequently talk about 'the way' and liken the Christian path to a journey. They have not yet reached their destination, but look to their religion to help them to do so.

The Christians' indistinguishable character is to be expected. In his highly important work *De Civitate Dei* ('City of God'), Saint Augustine (354–430) compares the world and the Church with two cities. There exists the 'earthly city', consisting of the worldly affairs in which we all participate, with its worldly values of wealth and pleasure, and there is the 'heavenly city', whose citizens belong to Christ's kingdom while continuing to belong to earthly society. While the 'heavenly citizens' are on earth, however, they cannot be distinguished from the purely 'earthly' ones. Augustine refers to a parable Jesus told about a farmer who planted wheat in his field, only to find that an enemy later sowed weeds (Matthew 13:24–9, 36–43). His servants offer to root them out, but the farmer prefers to wait until the harvest, when the good crops and the weeds will be more readily distinguishable. Jesus frequently uses the metaphor of a harvest to explain the kingdom of God: it is something that has small beginnings on earth, but will reach fruition at the end of time.

Traditionally, Christians have expected human history to culminate in Christ's return to earth. Luke reports that at Jesus' ascension 'two men dressed in white' appeared and reassured the disciples that 'This same Jesus, who has been taken from you into heaven, will come back in the same way you have seen him go into heaven' (Acts 1:11). Many Christians take this literally, expecting Jesus to return to earth on a cloud, in a literal physical way. Paul writes about an apocalypse in which Christ will descend from heaven, accompanied by angels, to the sound of a loud trumpet call. The 'dead in Christ' will rise first, then the living faithful ones will rise up to meet him in the air. This expected event is known as 'the rapture', particularly by Christian fundamentalists in the United States. Christians who are more liberal believe that there will be some culmination point to human history, but biblical texts about angels blowing trumpets and the Son of Man descending on the clouds are pieces of symbolic imagery, being attempts to explain ideas which, from an earthly standpoint, we cannot fully understand.

Chapter 2

Sources of Authority

The Christian's principal source of authority is Jesus Christ. Christ is the head of the Church, to which all Christians belong. Matthew's Gospel reports that people were amazed at Jesus' teaching 'because he taught as one who had authority, and not as their teachers of the law' (Matthew 7:29). He also recounts Jesus' final words to his disciples, 'All authority in heaven and on earth has been given to me' (Matthew 28:18). Jesus, as the Son of Man, has the final authority in adjudicating on who is fit to enter God's kingdom and who will be eternally excluded.

When Christians pray, they address their prayers to Christ, or to God the Father 'through Jesus Christ our Lord', and many believe that they hear Christ speaking to them – not usually in a literal sense, but through subtle signs, inner convictions or through the voice of their conscience. In recent times, a movement has grown up, particularly within evangelical Protestant circles, known as 'What Would Jesus Do?' (WWJD). The movement markets clothing and paraphernalia bearing this slogan, as a reminder to the Christian that imagining oneself in the position of Jesus will prove to be an effective guide to moral decision-making. Jesus, being the sinless human being, serves as a role model to the Christian.

Direct experiential claims have their problems, however. When former US President George W. Bush claimed that God had told him to invade Iraq, many Christians were sceptical. How does one distinguish between the voice of God and one's own imagination or wishful thinking? Christianity claims to have God's final revealed truth, and typically asserts itself as the sole means of salvation. It is therefore important to have some kind of means of assessing what is true and what is false in matters of doctrine and ethics. Christians typically acknowledge three main sources of authority, often in uneasy tension with each other: the Church, the Bible, and personal conscience. Protestantism regards the Bible as the supreme source of authority, and Calvinists have emphasized the principle of *sola scriptura* ('by scripture alone'). John Calvin (1509–64), the Protestant Reformer, contended that the Bible, acknowledged to be an infallible book, contained all that was necessary to gain salvation, and that sound doctrine and moral teaching must be thoroughly provable by reference to biblical sources. Catholic and Orthodox theologians point out, however, that the Bible is not primordial. The Church came into existence at Pentecost, when the only scriptures that Christians acknowledged were the Jewish ones, and it pre-dates the writing of even the first pieces of scripture, let alone the formation of the Christian canon. (The first piece of scripture is possibly Paul's letter to the Galatians, reckoned to have been written around 55 CE, and the Christian canon was probably agreed around 367 CE.) It was the Church that was responsible for defining which scriptures were to be regarded as normative, and hence the Church is the repository of the faith. According to Protestants, however, it is through the Bible that we are told how the Church began, and what its early teachings were: hence the Bible should be regarded as primordial.

There is common ground between the traditions insomuch as all of them acknowledge the authority of scripture, although, in addition to the Old and New Testaments, Roman Catholicism and the Orthodox Churches acknowledge the Apocrypha (called 'the longer canon' in Orthodoxy), which is a set of Jewish intertestamental writings. All Christians also accept the Church's early teachings, defined before it split into separate traditions. Thus, the Nicene Creed is accepted by the whole of Christendom, but Orthodoxy does not acknowledge the Apostle's Creed, since this was defined only by the Western Churches. (However, there is no clause in the Apostle's Creed with which Orthodox Christians would disagree.) The main bone of contention between the three traditions relates to papal authority. Protestantism rejects it entirely, while Orthodoxy acknowledges the authority of the Bishop of Rome, but only as one primate among several.

The Bible

The word 'Bible' (Greek, *biblos*) simply means 'book', and Christians are agreed that the scriptures of the Old and New Testament constitute the Word of God. These writings are believed to stand out from any other books, however inspiring these may be. They are inspired, rather than merely inspiring. The second letter to Timothy, attributed to Paul, states, 'All scripture is inspired by God, and profitable' (2 Timothy 3:16, RSV). The letter to Timothy was not, of course, referring to the entire Bible at that stage of the Church's – and the Bible's – development, but Christians today would regard the statement as true of their scriptures as a whole.

The Christian decision to incorporate all of the Jewish scriptures into their canon (authoritative writings) was the result of some careful debate. It might be wondered why the Christians should include within their scriptures ideas that they clearly rejected – in particular the requirements of Jewish law. Christianity was originally a Jewish sect, and in all probability Jesus had no intention of starting a new religion. The earliest Christians were Jews, and the first Christian community arose in Jerusalem. As teachings about Jesus spread, largely although not exclusively as the result of Paul's missionary activities, Gentiles as well as Jews came to accept Jesus as the messiah. This raised the question of whether Gentiles had to undergo circumcision as a means of entry to the Christian faith, and whether they had to observe requirements such as the Jewish dietary laws. Peter originally favoured the conservative stance, which was that the Christian faith was a distinctive form of Judaism: after all, many Jews were expecting a messiah, and Christianity was simply teaching that such expectations had now been fulfilled. Paul, however, took Peter to task for his conservatism, and, as a result, the Church decided that circumcision and the food laws could be abandoned (Acts 15:1–21). Much of Paul's writing argues against the view that salvation can be obtained through obedience to the Law.

When Christianity developed further, the question of whether Jewish scripture should be part of the Christian canon arose. Some early Christians, such as Marcion (c. 85–160), wanted to exclude it completely and accept only Paul's writings and those of Luke (who was a Gentile). However, the prevailing view among Christians was that the Jewish scripture points to Christ. If it is read with the eyes of faith, it is apparent that many Old Testament passages referred to Jesus Christ, although not by name. Isaiah, for example, writes about a 'suffering servant', who was without guilt, but who bore the sins of others (Isaiah 53:4–6). Jesus was himself a Jew, and it was important to portray him as the king over God's people. Hence the Gospel writers showed that he was descended from King David, born in

David's home city (Bethlehem), and that many of the references to kingship apply to Jesus. One example is Psalm 110:

> The LORD says to my Lord:
> 'Sit at my right hand
> until I make your enemies
> a footstool for your feet.'
> ...
> The LORD has sworn
> and will not change his mind,
> You are a priest for ever,
> in the order of Melchizedek.
>
> (Psalm 110:1, 4)

The New Testament writers themselves claimed to see these allusions. Luke says that Jesus applied this psalm to himself (Luke 20:41–4), and the writer to the Hebrews describes Jesus as the high priest of the Melchizedek priesthood (Hebrews 7:17).

There is certainly a close connection between Christianity and Judaism, and Christian scriptures would certainly make little sense without the Jewish ones. The Christian story is offered as a continuation and fruition of the Jewish one, and the New Testament contains many allusions to and quotations from the Old. Why Christians should adopt exactly the same writings as the Jews has no clear answer, particularly since the Jewish canon was formed in the Christian era, possibly in 90 CE, although some scholars have argued that it was even later.

The Old Testament consists of the following books: Genesis, Exodus, Leviticus, Numbers, Deuteronomy, Joshua, Judges, Ruth, 1 and 2 Samuel, 1 and 2 Kings, 1 and 2 Chronicles, Ezra, Nehemiah, Esther, Job, Psalms, Proverbs, Ecclesiastes, Song of Songs (a.k.a. Song of Solomon), Isaiah, Jeremiah, Lamentations, Ezekiel, Daniel, Hosea, Joel, Amos, Obadiah, Jonah, Micah, Nahum, Habakkuk, Zephaniah, Haggai, Zechariah, Malachi.

This is the order in which the books appear in the Western Churches. The Orthodox Churches have a slightly different ordering of the contents and slightly different nomenclature.

The first five books of Jewish scripture recount how the world was created, and the deeds of its early inhabitants. The first unarguably historical character to emerge is Abraham, who embarks on nomadic wanderings in search of a land that God has promised him. Abraham's descendants become slaves in Egypt, but escape captivity under Moses' leadership. The first five books, known to Jews as the Torah and to Christian scholars as the Pentateuch, also contain the Jewish laws. The book of Joshua tells of the Israelites entering the promised land of Canaan, and Judges recounts the new community's early leaders. The books of Samuel, Kings and Chronicles recount Israel's period as a monarchy, until they are invaded by Assyrians and Babylonians and taken captive. Ezra and Nehemiah were two Jewish leaders who organized the rebuilding of the Jerusalem Temple and Jerusalem's city walls after the people's release. Psalms, Proverbs and the Song of Solomon are Jewish poetry, while Job and Ecclesiastes are philosophical writings. The books from Isaiah to Malachi are prophetic writings, ending with the promise that God would send his messenger Elijah to herald 'the day of the Lord'.

The New Testament probably reached its current form around 367 CE. Various Christian leaders formulated slightly different lists of authoritative scriptural writings. Some early Christian writings were lost, while others were deliberately rejected. The Church was anxious to emphasize that Jesus Christ was the Son of God, both fully human and fully divine. Two early heresies the Church sought to combat were Docetism (the doctrine that Christ only seemed to be human, but was not really so) and Gnosticism (the belief that the acolyte had to ascend through layers of special knowledge to attain liberation from the present evil world to reach God's kingdom). Several pieces of writing, such as the apocryphal Gospels, told of childhood miracles of Jesus, which made him seem not wholly human, or portrayed him as disclosing esoteric teachings to his disciples. The Gospel of Thomas, discovered at Nag Hammadi in 1942, is a collection of sayings attributed to Jesus, secretly disclosed to the 12 apostles.

The New Testament consists of 27 books. They are: Matthew, Mark, Luke, John, Acts, Romans, 1 and 2 Corinthians, Galatians, Ephesians, Philippians, Colossians, 1 and 2 Thessalonians, 1 and 2 Timothy, Titus, Philemon, Hebrews, James, 1 and 2 Peter, 1, 2 and 3 John, Jude, Revelation.

The first four books are the four Gospels – accounts of Jesus' life and ministry. Acts is a continuation of Luke's Gospel, beginning with Jesus' ascension, the birth of the Church at Pentecost, and endeavours to propagate Christianity among the Gentiles, principally by Paul. The middle section of the New Testament, from Romans to Philemon, consists of letters attributed to Paul. Many Christians regard Paul as the author of Hebrews, a general piece of writing about Jesus' high-priestly role, although the book is in fact anonymous. James, Peter and John are letters to early Christian communities, purportedly by these three disciples of Jesus. Revelation is a rather enigmatic apocalyptic work, containing symbols and imagery that have proved to be difficult to unravel and that have given rise to many speculative interpretations. Its obscurity made some early Christians reluctant to include it within the canon, but it gained acceptance, being a piece of writing that offered encouragement to early Christians, who were victims of state persecution.

Although Christians hold the Bible to have authority, there is disagreement about precisely what such a claim means. For the fundamentalist, it means that the Bible is inerrant in all its aspects: its doctrines, its ethical requirements, its historicity. More liberal Christians find such a claim problematic. The Bible seems to contain contradictions, inaccuracies, and claims that conflict with science, and the Old Testament in particular seems to condone deeds that are considered quite unacceptable in our present-day society. For example, genocide seems to be condoned on more than one occasion (Joshua 10:28; 1 Samuel 15:3), many of the patriarchs and kings are polygamous, and some of the Old Testament penalties for alleged misdeeds, such as practising homosexuality, disobeying one's parents and breaking the sabbath, seem barbaric. Liberal Christians have no agreed alternative to belief in biblical inerrancy. Tom Wright, Bishop of Durham, itemizes several possible positions. Some claim that the Bible contains timeless truths; others that it witnesses the primary events that are instrumental in securing humanity's salvation; scholars like Rudolf Bultmann (1884–1976) suggest that it has a 'timeless function', continually calling men and women to decision. Wright's preferred explanation is that the Bible is a record of the 'word of God': God continually speaks, first to effect the world's creation, and subsequently to political leaders and to prophets. He compares the Bible to an unfinished play, where the playwright has written everything but the final scene, which we now have the task of completing (Wright, 1991, pp. 7–32). Viewed this way, God continues to speak his word to the Church.

The Roman Catholic stance on the authority of scripture is somewhat different: the authority of scripture and the authority of the Church are inextricably bound together. As Saint Augustine wrote, 'But I would not believe in the Gospel, had not the authority of the Catholic Church already moved me' (*Contra epistolam Manichaei*; quoted in *Catechism*, 119). The Bible is the 'sacred deposit' of the faith (*depositum fidei*), which means that it is the repository of the apostles' teaching, which it has recorded faithfully, and which the Church has the responsibility to transmit to each successive generation. It is God's speech through the Holy Spirit, and provides nourishment for the spiritual life. This does not mean that Roman Catholicism subscribes to a doctrine of literal inerrancy of scripture. On the contrary, there are Roman Catholic scholars who study and interpret the Bible critically, and who are entrusted with the responsibility for training the Church's clergy. The Church acknowledges that scripture is not always intended to be taken literally, and it distinguishes four senses in which scripture can be understood, according to context. There is a literal sense, for example where the biblical authors are attempting to record historical events, but there are three further 'spiritual senses' that can be discerned. First, there is an allegorical sense: events in the Old Testament can be regarded as cryptic allusions to Christ and the Christian faith. An example cited in the *Catechism of the Catholic Church* is Moses leading the Israelites across the Red Sea, where, as Paul explains, the allusion to water foreshadows the rite of baptism (Exodus 14; 1 Corinthians 10:2). Second, there is a 'moral sense', where conclusions regarding Christian behaviour can be deduced from the biblical narrative. Third, there is an 'anagogical sense', in which entities and events assume an eternal significance: the *Catechism* cites the example of the Church signifying the heavenly Jerusalem (*Catechism*, 115–18).

The Second Vatican Council declared that three criteria should be used in interpreting scripture. First, one must recognize 'the content and unity of the whole Scripture'. The Bible is no mere anthology: one part is to be understood in the light of another. As mentioned in the previous paragraph, the true meaning of the Old Testament cannot be perceived without the New. Second, scripture must be read in the context of 'the living Tradition of the whole Church' (*Catechism*, 113). The Church's insistence on being the custodian of scriptures is a safeguard against 'private interpretations': without the guidance of the tradition, a believer might alight on all manner of improbable interpretations of biblical passages. (One thinks of examples where authors have alleged that the Bible is about space aliens visiting the earth, or that it is an encoded document that predicted present-day world events. The Church as custodian of the sacred text ensures that the human imagination does not run riot.) Roman Catholicism does not accept the description that it is a 'book religion'. The Bible is only one source of authority, and the true source of authority is Christ himself. The *Catechism* quotes Hugh of St Victor (1096–1141), who wrote: 'All Sacred Scripture is but one book, and that one book is Christ, because all divine Scripture speaks of Christ, and all divine Scripture is fulfilled in Christ (*De arca Noe* 2, 8; quoted in *Catechism*, 134).

The Church as the bearer of authority has two interrelated aspects: the 'apostolic tradition' and 'ecclesiastical traditions'. When Jesus handed on his authority to Peter (Matthew 16:18–19), it is believed that he thereby initiated a line of tradition that would ensure that God's Word continued to be proclaimed in its authentic form. Being in the line of apostolic succession, the early Church Fathers, the saints, and leading thinkers such as Augustine and Thomas Aquinas (c. 1225–74) are typically cited as sources of authority, and their writings are to be interpreted rather than challenged.

The Church that has come down through this line of apostolic succession is episcopal in structure. The root meaning of 'episcopal' is 'overseeing' (Greek, *episcopē*), and in episcopal churches each member of the clergy has a superior to whom he is responsible, and whose instructions must be carried out. In Roman Catholicism, there is a hierarchy, with the Pope as the Supreme Pontiff, assisted by the Sacred College of Cardinals, who in turn oversee archbishops, bishops, and then priests. The Church's human authority is the Magisterium, which literally means 'teaching authority', and consists of all the clergy from the bishops upwards. It is held that, collectively, the Magisterium cannot provide false teachings, being the custodians of the faith of the apostles. It is the bishops who are the gatekeepers of the priesthood. For someone to become a priest, a bishop must perform the ordination; a priest cannot ordain another priest.

To the outsider, it can appear that the Roman Catholic Church is structured like a multinational organization, with the Pope as a kind of Chief Executive Officer, who line-manages his decisions through a Board of Directors down to the rank-and-file workers. This perception is no doubt encouraged by the doctrine of papal infallibility – a doctrine which is frequently misunderstood, particularly by Protestants. Belief in papal infallibility is not tantamount to holding that the Pope is either sinless, omniscient or inerrant, or that he makes pronouncements that are thereby binding on the Church. A papal pronouncement is only binding if it is *ex cathedra* – literally, 'from the throne'. There are three main conditions that must be satisfied for an *ex cathedra* pronouncement. First, it must provide 'solid teaching' – it cannot be about trivial matters. Second, it must concern faith or morals; the papal throne cannot be used to make political comment, for example. Third, the Pope must speak in his role as 'supreme universal pastor'. Just as monarchs do not normally sit on their thrones in private, but use them to receive officials and subjects, so the Pope's role as supreme universal pastor is not to act privately, but to sum up the authority of the Magisterium, and no pope would ever speak in such a capacity without being advised by his bishops and cardinals. The doctrine of papal infallibility was not formally defined until 1870 at the First Vatican Council, and since that time a pope has only once claimed such authority. This was Pope Pius XII, when he defined the Dogma of the Assumption on 1 November 1950. (This is the belief that, upon her death, the Virgin Mary was taken directly into heaven, leaving no physical remains. This was no new teaching, however, since pious Catholics have believed it for many centuries: the Pope was merely summing up authoritatively the Church's position.)

Tradition

The Church is the body that has created two thousand years of tradition, and it is Christian belief that the Church has continually been guided by the Holy Spirit. Jesus tells his disciples shortly before his death that, although he will not remain in the world much longer, he will send the Holy Spirit, who is the spirit of truth and 'when he, the Spirit of truth comes, he will guide you into all truth' (John 16:13). The Holy Spirit and the Church are particularly associated, as we have seen, and hence the Christian can be assured of the veracity of the Church's teaching, when a matter of faith or morals has been agreed by the whole Church. This is why great emphasis is placed in all three traditions on the work of the Church's early 'Ecumenical Councils'. These were bodies to which, at least in intention, bishops from the entire Christian world were invited, and which sought to discern truth from error, and to defining authentic Christian teaching. There were, in all, seven such Councils, which met from the fourth century up to the eighth. They were:

325	The Council of Nicaea
381	The Council of Constantinople
431	The Council of Ephesus
451	The Council of Chalcedon

553   The Second Council of Constantinople
680–1   The Third Council of Constantinople
787   The Second Council of Nicaea.

In the early centuries, doctrines that have come to be firmly associated with Christianity were still being worked out. In particular, the first four of these Councils addressed the question of how Jesus Christ could be fully God and fully human. To assign a dual role to someone is normally to assert that he or she is partly one and partly the other; for example a 'secretary-treasurer' has both functions, but not simultaneously or perpetually. One major problem concerning the doctrine of the Incarnation was that Christians wanted to claim that Jesus Christ was fully God and fully man, not a half-human half-divine hybrid, and not someone who sometimes fulfilled one role and sometimes the other. Moreover, Christians had given Jesus the title 'Son of God', but God is typically referred to as 'Father'. If Jesus Christ is God, how can the Father be the Son, and vice versa?

This was a problem to which Arius (c. 250–c. 336), a priest from Alexandria in Egypt, suggested a solution: Jesus Christ was 'of like substance' (Greek, *homoiousios*) with the Father, but not 'of the same substance' (*homoousios*). Thinking in terms of 'substances' was derived from the philosophy of Aristotle, who taught that every entity possesses an invisible 'substance' or 'essence' underlying its physical characteristics, which gives it its identity. As a rough analogy, one might consider a matching knife and a fork: both (let us assume) are made of steel, and thus they are 'of like substance', but not 'of the same substance' since the knife is not the fork. In philosophers' jargon they are 'qualitatively identical', not 'numerically identical'. This was roughly Arius' position regarding the relationship between God and Jesus Christ. Christ possesses many of the qualities of God: he existed before the world, was its creator, is wise, perfect, and worthy of worship; however, he is not co-eternal with God. As Arius reasoned, sons are born after their fathers, hence 'there was a time when he did not exist'.

Arius' position no doubt seemed very logical, but the Church has tended to resist rationalist solutions to theological problems. Athanasius, the Bishop of Alexandria, was particularly condemnatory of Arius. Since Christianity had become a powerful force within the Roman Empire, the Emperor Constantine I, who had himself converted to Christianity and legalized its practice, decided to convene a council to resolve the dispute. This assembly met at Nicaea in 325

CE, and marked a victory for Athanasius' supporters over the Arians. The Council formulated a creed – the Creed of Nicaea – which was a proto-version of the Nicene Creed, which continues to be acknowledged and recited by Christians today. The Nicene Creed, in its present-day form, emerged from the third of the Ecumenical Councils – the Council of Constantinople – which met in 381 CE. In the intervening period a number of related issues arose concerning the nature of Christ. Apollinarius (c. 310–c. 390), Bishop of Laodicaea, proposed that Christ had a divine mind and a human body, while Eutyches (c. 375–454), a priest at Constantinople, suggested that Jesus was born human, but was later divinized by God. These positions did not present Christ as being fully human and fully divine, and hence were rejected by the Councils of Constantinople and Chalcedon respectively.

Another early dispute related to the Virgin Mary. The Church had begun to refer to her as *theotokos*, meaning 'bearer of God'. Since Mary was the mother of Jesus, then, if Jesus is God, Mary must be the 'Mother of God'. Nestorius (c. 386–c. 451), Archbishop of Constantinople, perceived problems with this doctrine. If Jesus was fully God, then when Jesus was a child, God must only have been in his infancy also. Again, piety prevailed over strict logic, and the description 'Mother of God' still remains.

The creed that emerged from the deliberations at Chalcedon runs as follows.

We believe in one God,
the Father, the Almighty,
maker of heaven and earth,
of all that is,
seen and unseen.
We believe in one Lord, Jesus Christ,
the only Son of God,
eternally begotten of the Father,
God from God, Light from Light,
true God from true God,
begotten, not made,
of one Being with the Father;
through him all things were made.
For us and for our salvation he came down from heaven,
was incarnate from the Holy Spirit and the Virgin Mary
and was made man.

For our sake he was crucified under Pontius Pilate;
he suffered death and was buried.
On the third day he rose again
in accordance with the Scriptures;
he ascended into heaven
and is seated at the right hand of the Father.
He will come again in glory to judge the living and the dead,
and his kingdom will have no end.
We believe in the Holy Spirit,
the Lord, the giver of life,
who proceeds from the Father [and the Son],
who with the Father and the Son is worshipped and glorified,
who has spoken through the prophets.
We believe in one holy catholic and apostolic Church.
We acknowledge one baptism for the forgiveness of sins.
We look for the resurrection of the dead,
and the life of the world to come.
Amen.

A few points are worth highlighting. The Councils of Nicaea and Chalcedon were careful to state that Christ was 'eternally begotten' – a rebuttal of Arius' declaration that 'there was a time when he was not'. Jesus Christ is 'true God from true God', not some kind of God–man hybrid, or a semi-divine subordinate. He is 'of one Being [substance] with the Father', not 'of like substance'. Although the creed does not specifically mention that Mary is the *theotokos*, it declares that the Incarnation took place through Mary. Mary did not give birth to a mere human figure, who was later adopted by God as his Son.

A number of views concerning Christ are excluded by the ancient creeds. Mainstream Christianity rejects subordinationism – the belief that Christ is not equal with the Father (Arianism is one such example). It rejects adoptionism – the position that Christ was born human, but became divine: some Adoptionists have cited the baptism of Jesus as the occasion of Jesus' adoption, when the voice from heaven declared that Jesus was his Son. Monophytism is the belief that Jesus Christ had only one nature (either human or divine), while Monothelitism holds that Christ had two natures, but only a divine and not a human will. This last position was proscribed by the seventh of the Ecumenical Councils (the Second Council of Nicaea, 680–1): the Bible makes it clear that Jesus was subject to temptation, and that in the Garden of Gethsemane he agonized about doing his Father's will to the extent of facing death (Matthew 26:39). Few rank-and-file Christians would be familiar with the complexities of the debates surrounding Christ's person, although some of the ideas are conveyed through the liturgy and in hymns. Clergy are expected to be able to distinguish between orthodoxy and heresy, and could face disciplinary action for propounding false teaching. Unlike ancient times, heresy trials are now rare, although not entirely unknown.

The Nicene Creed does not explicitly state the doctrine of the Trinity, although God's triune nature is implicit in the creed's threefold division. Most mainstream Christians, and even members of the clergy, would hesitate to offer a coherent explanation of the Trinity, but the doctrine is well embedded in the Christian tradition. It is affirmed at various points in the liturgy, and frequent reference is made to the Father, Son and Holy Spirit in the Church's hymns. Churches seeking full membership of the World Council of Churches are expected to be Trinitarian in their theology (World Council of Churches, 2006). The doctrine affirms that God is fully and equally the Father, the Son and the Holy Spirit; the three are one, although each member is not identical with the others. If this sounds confusing, most Christians would agree that there is more than an element of mystery in the teaching, and that certain things are to be accepted as matters of faith.

Apart from the *filioque* clause, the Nicene Creed is accepted by all three major traditions. The Orthodox Churches acknowledge a number of aspects of tradition. Since 'tradition' literally means 'that which is passed on', the Holy Tradition encompasses a range of sources that pass on Christian belief and practice. These include the Bible, and the early Church Fathers. The latter includes names such as Irenaeus, Athanasius, Basil the Great, Gregory of Nyssa, and John Chrysostom, to name but a few. John Chrysostom was particularly renowned for his eloquent preaching ('Chrysostom' was a nickname, meaning 'gold mouth'), and the Liturgy of Saint John Chrysostom, which is widely used in Orthodox churches, is derived from Chrysostom's liturgical writings. Orthodox Christians are encouraged to read the writings of the Fathers. They are extensive, and quite difficult to read, and the guidance of a spiritual supervisor is recommended. The *Philokalia* is an anthology of spiritual writings containing a selection of the patristic writings.

Also included in the notion of Tradition in Orthodoxy is the use of icons. An icon is a flat image of Christ, the Virgin Mary, a saint, or a prophet, normally painted on wood. Their use today is not exclusive to Orthodoxy: they are frequently found in Roman Catholic churches, and in some Anglican ones. They are part of the Tradition because the artist must be a believer who leads a life of prayer and devotion; the icon should originate from the painter's heart, and must be approved by the church authorities. The painter's work is regarded as a continuation of the Incarnation, transforming the spiritual into material form. The faithful are encouraged to use icons rather than simply admire them, and many icons have been considerably worn away by the touch or kisses of worshippers. Icons are related to the Second Council of Nicaea (787 CE), which affirmed their importance:

> ... [J]ust as the figure of the precious and life-giving Cross, so also the venerable and holy images, as well in painting and mosaic as of other fit materials, should be set forth in the holy churches of God, and on the sacred vessels and on the vestments and on hangings and in pictures both in houses and by the wayside, to wit, the figure of our Lord God and Saviour Jesus Christ, of our spotless Lady, the Mother of God, of the honourable Angels, of all Saints and of all pious people. For by so much more frequently as they are seen in artistic representation, by so much more readily are men lifted up to the memory of their prototypes, and to a longing after them ...
> (Online Christian Library, 2009)

In addition to the Nicene Creed, Roman Catholics and Protestants acknowledge two other creeds: the Apostles' Creed and the Athanasian Creed. Despite their names, and even though they contain nothing that is theologically objectionable to them, these creeds are not acknowledged by the Orthodox Churches. Both took their rise in the West, although their precise origins are uncertain. Although allegedly compiled by the 12 apostles, the Apostles' Creed was not found in its present form until the twelfth century, and the Athanasian Creed originated in Gaul (southern France) some time between 281 and 428. Unlike the other creeds, the Athanasian Creed explicitly affirms the doctrine of the Trinity:

> And the Catholick Faith is this: That we worship on God in Trinity, and Trinity in Unity;
> Neither confounding the Persons: nor dividing the Substance.
> (*Book of Common Prayer*: 58)

Doctrines such as the Trinity are not to be found in Jesus' teaching or in the Bible, although some Christians argue that there are hints in the Old and New Testaments. Martin Luther believed that these later teachings were implicit in scripture. He wrote, 'What did the Fathers do except seek and present the clear and open testimonies of Scripture? (*Against Latomus*, 1521; quoted in Teigen, 1982, p. 148).

The Protestant Reformers added their own confessions of faith: the Heidelberg Catechism (1563), the Belgic Confession (1566) and the Canons of Dordt (1619) are accepted by many Protestant Churches in Europe. Among Protestants in Britain, the Westminster Confession of Faith (1646) was acknowledged. Throughout Protestantism, these act as 'subordinate standards' to the true standard of doctrine, which is the Bible. As with the Bible, some Protestants will interpret these statements of faith more liberally than others.

Apart from the Lutheran Churches, Protestants are not organized episcopally. They adopt various models for managing their affairs. The Church of Scotland, for example, is governed by a hierarchy of church courts, the highest being its General Assembly, which meets annually. Decisions by higher courts are binding on lower ones. In other denominations, such as the Baptists and Congregationalists, the seat of authority is the congregation itself. The United Reformed Church (URC) in Britain was formed in 1972 by a merger of English Congregationalists and the English Presbyterian Church, combining two somewhat different organizational structures. The URC in its present form retains its District Councils, Synods and General Assembly, but these bodies tend to make decisions in an advisory capacity only.

Finally, mention should be made of conscience as an authority. Unlike the Roman Catholic and Orthodox Churches, the Protestant Churches do not have canons – recorded decisions of councils, which become binding on the faithful. As has been mentioned, there is the Bible as a standard of authority, but scripture has to be interpreted, and it does not always give clear answers to moral dilemmas. In his letter to the Romans Paul writes of a 'law ... written on their hearts, their consciences also bearing witness' (Romans 2:15). Paul is referring to the Gentiles, who do not acknowledge the Jewish law as guidance for life. It is no excuse for them to plead ignorance of God's law, since their conscience should enable them to distinguish right from wrong. The role of conscience will be considered further in a later chapter; in the meantime, it should be noted that not all authority in Christianity is external, but that there is an important role for an inner authority, although conscience is not a *carte blanche* to justify any doctrine or behaviour.

Chapter 3

Science and Christianity

It is a popular conception that Christianity wants to roll back the clock and stem the tide of advancing science. The debate about 'Science and Religion' frequently becomes characterized as 'Science *versus* Religion'. One possible interpretation of the story of the Fall is that the prohibition on Adam and Eve to eat of 'the tree of the knowledge of good and evil' (Genesis 2:17) was a caution against acquiring new knowledge, good and evil being the totality of the universe's reservoir of what is known. Critics such as Richard Dawkins frequently seem to suppose that by promoting evolutionism against creationism one is undermining the foundations of the Christian faith.

It is important to set the record straight on such matters at the outset. A 1997 Gallup survey revealed that some 40 per cent of scientists are Christian, and there is a slight preponderance of Christians who accept evolutionary theory against creationism (51 per cent, according to Gallup 2004). Many famous scientists throughout history have been Christians, and Protestantism's Puritan strand was instrumental in the scientific progress of its time. The 'Creationism versus Evolutionism' debate does not pose a simple choice: both theories admit of different forms, indicating that there are different ways of relating the Christian faith to scientific advancement, ranging from conflict to integration. To confine the 'Science and Religion' debate to evolution would be unduly restricting. Christianity has reacted with science in a variety of ways, on a variety of issues. These include the possibility of miracles, the efficacy of prayer, whether religion is conducive to health and well-being, research in genetics and implications about the creation of life, and the implications of ecology on care of the earth's resources.

'Science and Religion' or 'Science versus Religion'?

The relationship between science and religion (or more specifically Christianity) is often presented in terms of polarized opposition. Christianity's detractors frequently portray the Church as anti-scientific, citing the example of its treatment of Copernicus and Galileo, its opposition to Darwin's theory of evolution, its belief in miracles, and apparently superstitious beliefs in sacred relics such as the Turin Shroud. Although the Church has not always reacted appropriately to scientific discovery, the notion that there is a conflict between reason and faith, or between science and the Bible, is largely the result of misunderstanding.

Ian G. Barbour (b. 1923) is an American physicist who went on to study divinity at Yale University, eventually becoming a professor of religion. His book *Issues in Science and Religion* (1965) effectively opened up the field, and is a standard work for undergraduates studying philosophy of religion. Barbour discusses issues such as the Big Bang, quantum physics, biological evolution and genetics. He contends that neither science nor religion have all the answers to the fundamental questions about the world. Scientists can tell us that there was a Big Bang that set the universe in motion, or define the laws governing our finely tuned universe. However, science cannot tell us why there is a universe at all, or why our universe is so finely tuned in the first place. Atheists who claim that this is due to chance, or that we live in one of a number of 'multiverses', are not making scientific pronouncements. They are equally speculating about the world, making philosophical conjectures.

Barbour distinguishes four different possible relationships between religion and science: conflict, independence, dialogue, and integration. The first is the kind that has surfaced in the creationist–evolutionist polarization. The second model suggests that religion and science describe different aspects of reality – the physical and the spiritual – and do not cross paths, having no common subject-matter. The third entails complementarity, with the scientist and theologian being able to put together different insights that will build up our conception of reality. It is the fourth model that Ian Barbour adopts, together with scientist-theologians John Polkinghorne (b. 1930) and Arthur Peacocke (1924–2006), both of whom will be discussed later in this chapter.

The Case of Galileo

One of the earliest interactions between science and religion was the Copernican revolution in astronomy. However, this was not an example of conflict between science and religion, but of Barbour's third model – complementarity. Neither Nicolaus Copernicus (1473–1543) nor Galileo Galilei (1564–1642) were opponents of the Church. Copernicus' astronomical observations and calculations, which he made throughout his lifetime, suggested to him that the earth orbited the sun, and not vice versa, as the previously held astronomical system of Ptolemy had suggested. Copernicus was hesitant to publish his findings, and only his *Commentariolus* ('Little Commentary') was published during his lifetime. Georg Joachim Rheticus, a mathematician from Wittenberg, encouraged him to publish what became his most influential work, *De revolutionibus orbium coelestium* ('Concerning the revolutions of the celestial spheres'). The Protestant Reformer Philipp Melanchthon (1497–1560) had sent Rheticus to Frombork, in Prussia, where Copernicus had settled. Rheticus, and subsequently the Lutheran theologian Andreas Osiander (1498–1552), arranged for the book to be printed. Legend has it that Copernicus was presented with a copy on his deathbed, where he awoke from his coma, looked at his book, and died peacefully.

The obvious problem that Copernican theory posed for Christianity was its apparent incompatibility with scripture. The Bible was written by flat-earthers who regarded the earth as the centre around which the stars and planets revolved, with humanity as the central point of God's creation. The Church's reluctance to accept the new theory was influenced by its understanding of several statements in the Bible, for example: 'The world is firmly established; it cannot be moved' (Psalm 93:1) and 'The sun rises and the sun sets, and hurries back to where it rises' (Ecclesiastes 1:5).

Those who were sympathetic to the new astronomy suggested ways of easing the tension. Osiander had prefaced *De revolutionibus* with an anonymous introduction in defence of its publication, supporting Copernicus' theory as facilitating astronomical calculations, rather than an attempt to define objective truth. Galileo later argued that one should not interpret such biblical passages literally, but allow for the presence of poetry and song within scripture. The new understanding of the world was not in hostile opposition to the Christian faith.

Copernicus died before the invention of the telescope in 1608. Galileo, who was born over twenty years after Copernicus' death, was able to make use of this piece of technology, and his observations impelled him to endorse heliocentrism publicly. In 1616, however, the Pope's theological advisers stated that the heliocentric view of the universe was unacceptable scientifically and was probably heretical. Cardinal Robert Bellarmine, who knew Galileo, advised him of this conclusion, and warned him against defending heliocentrism and interpreting scripture to harmonize with it. The Roman Catholic Church's Congregation of the Index suspended Copernicus' *De revolutionibus*, requiring 'corrections'; heliocentrism was perceived as threatening. Authorized by the Inquisition and by Pope Urban VIII, Galileo agreed to write a work that set out the arguments for and against the geocentric and heliocentric views of the world, but not to express his own opinions on the matter. The emergent work was his *Dialogue concerning the Two Chief World Systems* (1632). Although Galileo was instructed to set out the two competing views impartially, the *Dialogue* is set in the home of his friend Giovanni Sagredo, with Filippo Salviati, one of his students, championing heliocentrism. The proponent of geocentric conservatism is a fictitious 'Simplicio', who echoes some of Pope Urban VIII's own statements. It is unsurprising that Galileo was called to stand trial and sentenced to house arrest for the rest of his life. The *Dialogue* was banned.

It may seem puzzling that, just over a century later, Galileo's *Dialogue* was reinstated: in 1758 it was removed from the Vatican Index of forbidden books, and there was no prohibition on writings promoting heliocentrism. The ban remained on uncensored versions of Copernicus and Galileo's writings, although even that was dropped in 1835. A number of points must be noted about the Church and the revolution in astronomy. First, there was no polarization between the Church and the scientists. Copernicus, Galileo and their students belonged to the Church and never abandoned their faith. The Church was not opposed to science; indeed Copernicus was a priest, and a canon at Frombork Cathedral. Second, Galileo's trial was a disciplinary one, not a heresy trial, and at no time did the Roman Catholic Church declare heliocentrism to be contrary to the Church's teachings. Copernicanism was never defined as heretical either by a Pope or by a Church council. In fact, the Church was quite amenable to the new astronomical theories being entertained as hypotheses. What the Church was not prepared to accept was that heliocentrism was a proven fact, as Galileo had tried to insist. This brings us to the third point: that in the sixteenth and seventeenth centuries heliocentrism appeared simply to be bad science, lacking conclusive proof and leaving several questions unanswered. It was not until a century and a half later that the Copernican view of the universe was established with certainty. Fourth, the Church has supported scientific advance, before and after Galileo, including research in astronomy, and no *volte face* was involved in finally acknowledging that Copernicus and Galileo's theories proved superior to Ptolemy's system.

Neither the Roman Catholic Church nor Galileo handled the situation well, however. The Church was undoubtedly heavy-handed in its approach, and Galileo tactless in the extreme. In an attempt to set records straight, Pope John Paul II set up a pontifical commission in 1981 to study the Ptolemaic–Copernican controversy. The commission, which concluded that the Church had persecuted Galileo but was not wholly blameworthy, heralded a move within the Church to honour Galileo. In 2008 an anonymous donor offered funds for a statue of Galileo to be installed at the Vatican's Pontifical Academy of Sciences. The following year, 2009, was the International Year of Astronomy, and Pope Benedict XVI sent greetings to the participants, stating unequivocally his support for astronomical advance. A special exhibition was mounted in the Vatican Museum to celebrate the year.

Creationism versus Evolution

The Protestant fundamentalist response to Darwin did not proceed in the way the Copernican revolution did. Many liberal Christians successfully integrated evolutionary theory with Christianity, but the fundamentalist response, particularly in the United States, was confrontational. The theory of evolution was perceived as a threat to Christianity for several reasons. First, it seemed to run counter to the account of the six-day creation. Instead of creating Adam on the sixth day of the world's existence, the theory implied that humanity's coming into being was the result of a lengthy process, spanning millions of years. Second, the Bible suggests that *homo sapiens* was a special creation by God, singled out from other species, with the special responsibility of exercising dominion over the other species. Evolutionism implied that humanity was not created specially with a specific purpose, but was a life form that was continuous with other species, principally apes. Third, by claiming that the evolution of species involved natural selection and the survival of the fittest, Darwin and his supporters seemed to imply that the creative process was wasteful, with some life forms coming into existence and dying swiftly because they were ill adapted to their environment. This waste seemed improvident and incompatible with the notion of a benevolent God who had a clear purpose for his creatures. Generally, Darwinism cast aspersions on the veracity of scripture, which had been regarded as an infallible source of authority in the pre-Enlightenment period.

There was a further problem that evolutionism posed. Evolutionism ran counter to an argument that had been characteristically used to demonstrate God's existence: the Argument from Design. The argument remains a popular one, and is often invoked in tracts that continue to be offered in town and city centres by street evangelists. The argument is frequently associated with William Paley (1743–1805). Paley's argument was that, if we were walking across a field and found a watch, we would immediately recognize it as a human artefact, designed for a purpose, unlike a stone, which is known to occur naturally. Phenomena in the universe – Paley takes the human eye as his example – display much greater intricacy than a watch, and have a definite purpose. It is therefore reasonable to conclude that there must be a 'divine watchmaker' who is responsible for the universe and the wonderful things that it contains.

The argument continues to arouse debate among philosophers of religion, some of whom have devised new and more complex versions in an attempt to surmount some of its problems. It is not our present task to consider these, but rather to examine how evolutionary theory impinged on Paley's argument. Darwin's theory offered a competing explanation to that of divine authorship, which the Church had championed throughout the centuries. Life forms with eyes that saw less clearly than others would more readily be prey for predators, and hence not the fittest to survive. Natural selection would weed them out, leaving in existence creatures with better eyes, of the kind at which Paley and others marvelled.

Creationist Responses

Evolution elicited a variety of responses from Christians. The first type of response was Creationism, which was essentially a rejection of Darwin's idea. Creationists reassert the inerrancy of scripture, and particularly the Book of Genesis' account of creation, against Darwinism. Creationism is not a monolithic theory, however, but assumes a variety of forms. Its most conservative form is typically called the Young Earth Theory, on account of its conviction that the earth is less than 10,000 years old. This chronology is based on that of Bishop James Ussher (1581–1656), Anglican Archbishop of Armagh, who made calculations from biblical statements about ages and dates, reaching the conclusion that the world was created on 22 October 4004 BCE. Ussher even specified the time: six o'clock in the evening. (This precision is not as ridiculous as might first be thought. Ussher reasoned that the world's first day must have been the first day of the Jewish New Year, and that the Jewish day began in the evening. The Book of Genesis mentions the evening before the morning: 'And there was evening, and there was morning – the first day' (Genesis 1:5).) Young Earth Creationists hold that there was a single creative event, *ex nihilo* ('out of nothing'), and that all life forms were created directly by God, with no subsequent evolutionary development taking place, and no new organisms coming into existence. Young Earth Creationists deny the existence of 'transitional fossils' – fossils that purport to be hybrids between species, such as 'missing links' between apes and humans – and are eager to point out that findings such as the Piltdown Man and the Nebraska Man were hoaxes. Literal acceptance of the world's early history, as recounted in Genesis, involves belief in the story of Noah and a flood which enveloped a large area of the world. Young Earth Creationists claim that such a flood explains phenomena such as sedimentary layers and fossils in the earth's geological structure, as well as the existence of fossil fuels. Supportive evidence is also found in the fact that other cultures and religions recount ancient flood stories. This variety of Creationism entails that the Bible is scientifically as well as historically accurate. When professional scientists do not support Young Earth Creationism, these Creationists then demand that one makes the choice between accepting the Bible or accepting science, adopting a 'Religion versus Science' stance.

Old Earth Creationism, as the name suggests, rejects the idea that the earth is less than 10,000 years old, typically putting its age at around four billion years. (Non-creationist scientists reckon that the 'Big Bang' occurred 13.75 billion years ago.) It also rejects 'flood geology' – the theory that an ancient flood explains geological phenomena. There are different justifications for postulating an older earth than that suggested by the Young Earth Creationists, and these generate at least two forms of Old Earth Creationism: Gap Creationism, and Progressive Creationism.

Gap Creationism is so called because of a belief that between the events related in the first and second verses of the first chapter of

Genesis, we are to understand that a 'gap' occurred of several billion years. The first verse states plainly that 'In the beginning God created the heaven and the earth', as if God created the earth instantaneously out of nothing, but subsequent verses go on to recount how God created the world out of a watery chaos. The Scofield Reference Bible (1909), which supports a Gap Creationist view, inserts 'Earth made waste and empty by judgment' between the two verses, citing Jeremiah 4:23–26. Jeremiah refers to a total destruction of the earth through divine judgement, and the editors suggest that this judgement may be associated with the angelic Fall. God's destruction of the world requires a new creative act, the account of which commences at the second verse. The 'gap' theory thus allows the earth to be sufficiently old for genuine fossils and other geological phenomena to have formed: 'The first creative act refers to the dateless past, and gives scope for all the geologic ages' (Scofield, 1909, p. 3).

An alternative form of Old Earth Creationism is Progressive Creationism, also known as 'Day Age' Creationism. The earth's age is explained, not by a 'gap' requiring the earth's reconstitution, but because the word 'day' in the Bible does not necessarily mean a 24-hour period. Several Protestant Reformers, such as John Wycliffe (c. 1330–84), Martin Luther (1483–1546), and John Calvin (1509–64), used a 'day-for-a-year rule' for interpreting biblical prophecy. This rule is still used by Adventists and by Jehovah's Witnesses in determining end-time calculations. This theory rests on the belief that God operates on a different time-scale from mortals, and that his 'days' are substantially more extended than ours. A number of biblical citations are held to bear this out; for example, 'For a thousand years in your sight are like a day that has just gone by, or like a watch in the night' (Psalm 90:4). The six 'days' of creation therefore signify a much longer passage of time than a literal interpretation of the word 'day' suggests, and thus the creation story is about a gradual creation, allowing for natural processes to take place, and even for limited gene mutation and evolutionary development ('micro-evolution') within species. Some Progressive Creationists acknowledge that members of the cat family bear resemblances that suggest a possible common origin, and that birds' beaks have adapted to their environments. It is also acknowledged that species become extinct. However, there is no 'transitional evolution' whereby a species evolves into another or a new species comes into existence. The creation story indicates an overall framework in which the creative process took place, with God having direct control over each stage.

Intelligent Design

A further recent position on evolution is Intelligent Design (ID). It is sometimes called Neo-Creationism, although many of its supporters prefer to get away from terminology that includes the word 'Creationism'. The movement gained momentum in the mid- to late 1980s, largely replacing the terms 'Creation Science' and 'Scientific Creationism', following certain legal battles that the Creationists lost earlier in that decade relating to the teaching of Creationism in schools. The First Amendment of the US Constitution requires that no state aid be given to religion, and hence that religious doctrines should have no part in school education. Concerned that this situation favoured evolutionism, being a secular theory, the name 'Creation Science' was adopted by opponents of evolution, so that Creationism might be taught under the guise of science rather than religion. In 1981 the state of Arkansas determined that 'Creation Science' should be granted equal teaching time in state schools to theories of evolution. Creation Science was defined as:

(1) Sudden creation of the universe, energy and life from nothing.
(2) The insufficiency of mutation and natural selection in bringing about development of all living kinds from a single organism.
(3) Changes only with fixed limits of originally created kinds of plants and animals.
(4) Separate ancestry for man and apes.
(5) Explanation of the earth's geology by catastrophism, including the occurrence of a worldwide flood.
(6) A relatively recent inception of the earth and living kinds.

(Arkansas Act 590)

The Arkansas Board of Education had been persuaded by Christian fundamentalists to introduce this policy, but it was unwelcome in more liberal circles, and challenged by a number of secular as well as religious organizations. The legal challenge was headed by Methodist minister William McLean. On 5 January 1982, the judge, William Overton, ruled that Creation Science was not scientific, and outlined a number of criteria that a discipline must satisfy in order to count as a science. It must invoke natural law in its explanations; it must be empirically testable; and it must be open to challenge and possible falsification, not claiming to offer final unyielding conclusions. Creation Science, he ruled, satisfied none of these criteria, and thus

Creation Science must be regarded as religious, not scientific. This ruling was only binding on the State of Arkansas, but it seriously damaged the status of Creation Science in school curricula.

The crisis point for the teaching of Creation Science came in 1987, when the case of *Edwards v. Aguillard* came before the US Supreme Court. The litigation was a challenge to the State of Louisiana, whose education policies required the teaching of Creation Science as a legitimate alternative to evolution. The judge ruled that the State's policy infringed the Establishment Clause of the First Amendment, on the basis of three principles known as the Lemon Test (so named after a plaintiff in a 1971 legal case):

(1) the government's action must have a legitimate secular purpose;
(2) the government's action must not have the primary effect of either advancing or inhibiting religion; and
(3) the government's action must not result in an "excessive entanglement" of the government and religion.

(Lemon v. Kurtzman, 403 U.S. 602 (1971))

Faced with this fatal blow to Creation Science on the school curriculum, fundamentalists sought to redefine Creationism, developing the theory of Intelligent Design. The term was first applied in 1989 to this refurbished version of Creationism, although one can find earlier uses, including Darwin himself in a letter written in 1861. The year 1989 marked the publication of a book entitled *Of Pandas and People*, by Percival Davis and Dean H. Kenyon. The book was published by the Foundation of Thought and Ethics (FTE), a conservative Christian organization whose aims are defined as 'publishing, preaching [and] teaching ... the Christian Gospel and understanding of the Bible and the light it sheds on the academic and social issues of the day'. Work began on the book in 1982, and the text incorporated the term 'Creationism'. Charles B. Thaxton, the editor, ensured that the word was progressively removed, and the term 'Intelligent Design' substituted.

Intelligent Design theory, in reality, differs little from Creation Science. It rejects evolution and natural selection, contending that natural explanations are insufficient to account for the origins of life and the existence of different species. Most Intelligent Design proponents believe in Young Earth theory, although the precise age of the earth is an open question. The most significant departure from

Creation Science is the preference of ID supporters to avoid terms like 'God' and 'Creationism', claiming that ID theory leaves open the question of the precise nature of the universe's designer. The theory purports to be empirical, drawing on the evidence of design in the universe, which they believe far surpasses in complexity the design to which Paley drew attention. DNA, for example, is much more complex even than the human eye. Particular emphasis is given to the notion of 'irreducible complexity'. The term originates from Michael Behe, author of *Darwin's Black Box* (1996, rev. edn 2006), which he defines as 'a single system which is composed of several interacting parts that contribute to the basic function, and where the removal of any one of the parts causes the system to effectively cease functioning'. One of Behe's favourite examples of 'irreducible complexity' is a mouse trap. A mouse trap that lacked any one of its parts would not function at all; it would not merely be an inferior proto-version of a trap. Hence it could not evolve from something inferior, but must have a designer. Similarly, many features of the universe have an even greater irreducible complexity that suggests design, and not evolution. Behe cites the bacterial flagellum of *E. coli*, the blood-clotting cascade, and the adaptive immune system.

Intelligent Design supporters, however, have failed to convince the scientific and legal world that their account of the origins of life is truly scientific. Their theories have been rejected by the US National Academy of Sciences and the (US) Natural Science Teachers' Association. In 2005, 11 parents brought an injunction against the Dover Area School District, Pennsylvania, regarding its requirement that when evolution theory was taught Intelligent Design be identified as an alternative, and that students be directed to *Of Pandas and People* as a source of reference. Judge Jones, giving his opinion, stated that 'ID is a religious view, a mere re-labeling of creationism, and not a scientific theory' and that 'the writings of leading ID proponents reveal that the designer postulated by their argument is the God of Christianity' (Irons, 2007, pp. 60–87).

Inviolable Laws and Miracles

Science proceeds on the assumption that there are inviolable laws of nature governing the universe. This does not mean that scientists have yet discovered all of these, or that they cannot undergo modification to accommodate discrepancies. Although quantum physicists affirm that the behaviour of atomic particles is random, it is still possible to predict what will happen in the world at a macro-level, and the behaviour of atomic particles, as well as human behaviour, as investigated in the social and life sciences, can be assigned degrees of probability, which can be measured. Christians affirm that, when God created the world, he set it up with reliable, indeed unalterable laws. If God has set up the universe in this way, it may seem as if there is no room for divine interference. If God has created the universe well, then why should he need to intervene to change the way it is working, performing miracles? If the laws of nature are universal and unalterable, then how can they admit of exceptions? These are the kinds of questions that continue to be debated among philosophers of religion, who remain divided on the issue. Belief in miracles is not a requirement of faith, or necessary for salvation, although the ancient creeds make reference to events that many Christians would claim to be miraculous, such as the Virgin Birth and Christ's resurrection.

The majority of Christians believe in miracles. A survey in the United States in 2007 revealed that 86 per cent of Protestants (88 per cent of evangelicals), 83 per cent of Roman Catholics, and 79 of Orthodox Christians agreed with the statement, 'Miracles occur today as they did in ancient times' (Pew Forum, 2007). The Roman Catholic Church teaches that there are Christians to whom God has given special graces, or 'charisms', of which the ability to work miracles is one. In practice the number of Catholics claiming such powers is very few. One modern example is Padre Pio (1887–1968), who reportedly produced stigmata (marks appearing on one's body, resembling Christ's crucifixion wounds), and to whom many of the faithful flocked, believing that he had the ability to heal afflictions. Spiritual healing is more common within Protestantism, where faith healers are found, particularly in evangelical circles, as well as those who claim to perform 'deliverance ministries' – the ability to cast out demons. Roman Catholics are more inclined to associate miracles with saints and with shrines, the most famous of which is Lourdes.

There are many Christians who firmly believe that there are people who have the spiritual gifts of healing or working other kinds of miracles. Some do it in a modest, unpretentious way; for example, it is not uncommon for a Pentecostalist service to end with an invitation to members of the congregation to come forward for the laying on of hands for spiritual healing. There are other higher-profile healers who undertake international healing ministries, drawing crowds, and claiming spectacularly successful cures. Such evangelists include Morris Cerullo and Benny Hinn, although these ministries are highly controversial among Christians.

Science and Education

The theory of evolution, combined with the scientific advance of the nineteenth century, suggested the instrumentality of science in human progress. Could science be expected to take over from religion as a means of explaining the world and controlling human affairs? A number of scientists and philosophers believed so. In previous centuries the Church had controlled education, dominating prestigious universities such as Oxford and Cambridge. It was not until 1886 that it became possible to study science as a special degree at Oxford. Scientific projects such as Darwin's had been privately funded, and members of the public who were interested in furthering their knowledge of the sciences might attend evening classes at Mechanics' Institutes or read about scientific discoveries in popular magazines.

As the prestige of the sciences grew, affairs began to change, as some prominent thinkers began to call into question the role of religion in defining and explaining reality. Human knowledge had to evolve too, and theories that were unable to adapt to the changing intellectual climate ran the risk of becoming extinct. In his presidential address to the British Association for the Advancement of Science in 1874, John Tyndall said:

> The impregnable position of science may be described in a few words. We claim, and we shall wrest from theology, the entire domain of cosmological theory. All schemes and systems which thus infringe upon the domain of science must, in so far as they do this, submit to its control, and relinquish all thought of controlling it. Acting otherwise proved always disastrous in the past, and it is simply fatuous today. Every system which would escape the fate of an organism too rigid to adjust itself to its environment must be plastic to the extent that the growth of knowledge demands. (Tyndall, 1874, pp. 66–97)

The view that denied the existence of any metaphysical reality and asserted that there is nothing that is not amenable to empirical scientific investigation was known as 'Positivism'. Secular philosophers like John Stuart Mill (1806–73) advanced a secular form of morality that was independent of religion. His moral theory, utilitarianism, asserted that it is human pleasure and pain that are the real criteria of ethical thinking, rather than divine decree or God-given conscience. The English mathematician and philosopher W. K. Clifford (1845–79) contended that the mind is simply a complex arrangement of matter, and that morality is no more than what is conducive to one's social group.

The 'Prayer Gauge' Debate

One particular topic that aroused considerable debate was prayer. Between 1831 and 1849 the Privy Counsel in Britain had declared special days of prayer for the prevention of cholera. However, in 1853 Lord Palmerston, the Prime Minister, rejected such a call, insisting that sanitation was the answer, not prayers for divine protection or intervention. The Bishop of Oxford continued to hold that prayer was efficacious, eliciting responses from God and having the potential to alter events in the world. In 1860 he instructed the clergy to pray for good weather, contending that the summer's persistent rain, which hampered harvesting, was a divine judgement on the population. Five years later, rivalry between the Church and the scientists resurfaced with the outbreak of a cattle plague. The Archbishop of Canterbury composed a special prayer for deliverance, with the entreaty, 'Stay, we pray Thee, this plague by Thy word of power (Barsham *et al.*, 1987, p. 40). Meanwhile, Lyon Playfair, a prominent scientist, headed a Royal Commission, bringing the plague under control by slaughtering some of the animals.

Controversy between the Church and the scientists came to a head in 1871 when the Prince of Wales contracted typhoid and his life was in jeopardy. Sunday 10 December was declared a national day of prayer; by Thursday his condition had improved, and a service of thanksgiving for his recovery was held at St Paul's Cathedral. None of the nation's prominent scientists were invited. John Tyndall and Henry Thompson, a London surgeon, suggested that claims about the efficacy of prayer could be resolved by a scientific experiment. One ward in a hospital should be selected, in which patients would be systematically prayed for during a period of between three and five years, or even more. Their progress could be compared with a control group of patients from another ward, who received no such attention.

The media gave great publicity to the proposal, and there was much discussion among scientists, Church leaders and the general public, although the experiment itself was not carried out at the time. Articles on the topic from *The Contemporary Review*, *The Fortnightly Review* and *The Spectator* were collated and published in 1876.

The first investigator to collect data attempting to correlate prayer and human welfare was Francis Galton (1822–1911), a cousin of Charles Darwin, an early anthropologist and one of the first to apply statistical information to differences among human beings. His article 'Statistical Enquiries into the Efficacy of Prayer' was published in *The Fortnightly Review* in 1872. Galton reckoned that reigning monarchs were probably prayed for more than any other category of person. The *Book of Common Prayer* includes prayers for the Royal Family at every Morning Prayer, Evensong and Holy Communion. We should therefore expect royalty to be substantially healthier and to live longer than members of other professions. Galton concludes that the differences among the various professions are slight, and that monarchs do not come top, but in fact bottom. The average age to which male members of the royal family lived was 64.04, compared with 67.31 (the next higher), which was the average of medical practitioners as well as English aristocracy. Landed gentry came top at 70.22, closely rivalled by clergy at 69.49. Galton suggested mischievously that perhaps the clergy's success lay in their life of prayer, rather than their being the subjects of prayer.

In more recent times attempts at empirical studies of the effects of prayer have been undertaken, more along the lines of the proposed 1872 prayer-gauge experiment, which never materialized. These studies commenced in the late 1980s, mainly in the US Bible Belt. One recent estimate indicates that there have been at least 1,600 such studies (Dossey, 2001), which raises the question why so many are thought to be necessary. Most of the studies involved randomizing the names of hospital patients and assigning them indiscriminately to two groups, one of which would be prayed for by a team of Christian intercessors, and another merely given 'usual care'. None of these research projects reported spectacular cures, although one survey (Harris *et al.*, 1999) claimed that their intercessory group fared 11 per cent better than the 'usual care' group, measured against a number of medical criteria. Not all researchers are convinced by these findings, and other studies have found no significant difference. A team of researchers that examined 14 major controlled research projects of this type, concluded:

There is no scientifically discernible effect for intercessory prayer as assessed in controlled studies. Given that intercessory prayer literature lacks a theoretical or theological base and has failed to produce significant findings in controlled trials, we recommend that further resources not be allocated to this line of research.

It is not merely scientists who have found difficulties with these studies. Many Christians themselves find it problematic to believe that petitioning God can make a different to the recovery of specific people. Why should God cause some people to recover and not others? Why does he have to wait for someone to pray before effecting (or not effecting) a cure? Why should God allow people to fall ill in the first place? Christians have various answers to such questions, of course. Some Christians attribute disappointing results of prayer to one's inability to pray properly. Prayer is a skill that needs to be learned. As the *Catechism of the Catholic Church* states: 'Prayer cannot be reduced to the spontaneous outpouring of interior impulse: in order to pray, one must have the will to pray. Nor is it enough to know what the Scriptures reveal about prayer: one must also learn how to pray' (*Catechism*, 2650).

Protestants too offer training in prayer. Many books have been written on how to pray effectively, and there is no shortage of courses and resources on 'secrets of powerful prayer' and similar titles.

A different approach to prayer is that it is best understood, not as a set of instructions to God, with which he may or may not comply, but a means of placing one's concerns, holding up one's ideals before him, and attuning oneself to his will. Although Christians regularly pray for peace, justice, the healing of the sick, the safety of travellers, and the salvation of the world, most Christians would be astounded if all these benefits were granted in the course of the ensuing week, or even within their lifetimes!

The Turin Shroud

Another area in which religious claims have been subjected to scientific scrutiny is the famous Shroud of Turin. This shroud, bequeathed to Pope John Paul II in 1983, is housed within Turin Cathedral and is purportedly the linen shroud in which Jesus was buried (John 19:40). Pilgrims who visit the shroud do not typically claim to receive miracles from it: the shroud itself is regarded as the miracle. A human face and body appears to be imprinted on this cloth, and the man's wrists are believed to have wounds consistent with the piercing that occurred at the crucifixion. The forehead and scalp appear to be punctured, perhaps from the crown of thorns that the Roman soldiers placed on Jesus' head, and blood is visible on both arms. The history of the shroud can be traced with some certainty to 1349 when Geoffroi de Charny, a French knight, escaped from the English, bringing the shroud with him. There are many who believe that the shroud's origins are much older, and it is conjectured that the Shroud of Turin is the Image of Edessa (now Urfa in Turkey), referred to by the early church historian Eusebius of Caesarea (c. 260–c. 340) and brought to Constantinople in 944, but now lost. When the shroud was first photographed in 1898, the printed picture looked more like a photographic negative, causing accusations of forgery to be made against the photographer Secondo Pia. However, subsequent photography produced similar results, causing some believers (not all) to speculate that the image was caused by the energy released from Jesus' body as he passed through the grave-clothes at his resurrection. If this were the case, then the shroud attests to Christianity's most important miracle. The shroud was first seen on television in 1973, with a pre-recorded introduction by Pope Paul VI.

In the same year, permission was granted for samples of the shroud to be taken for scientific analysis. No doubt one important motive for this was the hope of rebutting sceptics, who dismissed the shroud as stemming from medieval superstition, but there was also the belief that faith and devotion should not be at odds with science. In 1976 pollen findings on the shroud indicated that it had been in contact with plants that were exclusive to Israel, suggesting that the shroud had been there at some point in its history, and thus providing confirmatory, although not conclusive, evidence of its authenticity. The following year, permission was given for carbon-14 dating to be carried out, although experiments did not commence for a further decade. Samples were taken and analysed by scientists working independently at Zurich, Arizona and Oxford. When the results were made public, they were unfavourable; on 26 August 1988 the *London Evening Standard* carried headlines stating that the shroud was a 'fake', dating from around 1325.

These scientific findings have by no means closed the matter. The methods and results of the teams of scientists have been challenged, not merely by pious devotees, but by scientists writing in peer-reviewed journals. Criticisms have included the possibility that the samples came from a rewoven area of the cloth and not the original shroud, that different samples yielded significantly different results, and that carbon monoxide in the atmosphere could have contaminated the shroud, seriously affecting the experiment (Rogers, 2005, pp. 89–194). It may seem as if this is an example of religion and science being at odds, with the believer refusing to accept the findings of science when they become unsupportive. This is not how the shroud controversy is viewed within the Church. The shroud still remains an enigma, whatever its date of origin, and Catholic scholars clearly distinguish between myth and potential truth. For example, they do not endorse the legend that the shroud was brought to Edessa by the apostles Thomas or Thaddaeus. From the scientists' viewpoint, the criticisms of the research have served to highlight the possibility of carbon-14 dating errors, and helped to make science more robust. Officially the Roman Catholic Church has made no pronouncement about the shroud's authenticity, which is a matter for individual judgement.

Scientist-theologians

Science-and-religion debates are not all about trying to reconcile scientific claims with Christianity or about attempts to verify or falsify Christian beliefs through science. Conscious of the fact that many scientists are religious, and many religious believers are also scientists, Arthur Peacocke had the vision of establishing a 'guild' of 'priest-scientists' – men and women in holy orders who would have a special concern for the ways in which science and religion interact. The Society of Ordained Scientists was set up in 1986 as a 'dispersed religious order' and has a membership of over eighty well-qualified scientists – spanning chemistry, physics, medical science and engineering – who have entered the priesthood or ministry. Members of the Order seek to support one other in their professions, and to assist the Church in its commitment to science and technology and their impact upon the world.

Two other scientist-theologians have gained particular prominence in addition to Ian G. Barbour: John Polkinghorne, and Arthur Peacocke. (There is also Paul Davies, whose book *The Mind of God* gained public attention. However, Davies does not align himself with the Christian faith.) Polkinghorne's theology derives from the nature of the universe, as defined by particle physics. We can no longer accept a mechanistic universe, consisting of solid matter that is governed by unfailing universal laws, into which perhaps God sometimes breaks to perform the occasional miracle. The universe's constituents are quarks and gluons, which cannot be observed physically and whose behaviour is unpredictable. They are not 'solid', and are not even observable with the most powerful microscope. Rather, they act as models, explaining the events that are observable at the macro-level. Unlike the Newtonian model of the universe, which deals with 'matter', suggesting 'mind–matter' and 'God–world' dichotomies, Polkinghorne argues that the world of atomic physics reflects the mind of the creator, and hence that gaining insight into science gains us insight into the mind of God. He describes his position as 'dual-aspect monism': there are not two realities (God and the world), but one reality that can be experienced in two different ways: by the believer and by the scientist. The world is not something that was triggered off by a single episodic divine action, either six thousand years ago, or 13.75 billion years previously. Rather, God's creation is continuous rather than a 'top down' causality.

Polkinghorne is particularly fascinated by the Anthropic Principle. This relates to the observation that the earth is 'fine-tuned' for supporting human life. The existence of a habitable environment depends on several factors that appear to be independent of each other: electrons' energy states, the level of nuclear force, the age of the earth, its chemical composition (especially the presence of carbon, oxygen and water). The Anthropic Principle was first introduced by theoretical physicist Brandon Carter in a paper presented in 1973. Paul Davies has elsewhere referred to it as *The Goldilocks Enigma* – the title of his recent book, which discusses the possible reasons for the conditions on earth being 'just right' for human life to exist. Carter's observation has now given rise to an enormous amount of debate among scientists, religious believers and critics of religion. The Principle has gone through various formulations, with differing claims regarding its significance. Although it does not restore humanity to its assumed central position in the universe, it seems to suggest that we have a privileged position. Since there is no other planet that we know of that sustains anything resembling human life, does this suggest that there is a creator God from whom the world originates? Many Creationists have welcomed the argument, although the Anthropic Principle, in its acknowledgment that the universe is 13.75 billion years old, amply allows for the evolution of species. It is unlikely, however, that the universe as a whole evolved into the state required to support intelligent life, since a process of random development of its individual components would have required a much longer time-frame. A number of scientists have suggested the idea of 'multiverses': perhaps there are many parallel universes that have developed over billions of years, and we merely inhabit one of them. If this were the case, then the fact that we live in a habitable universe would not be so remarkable. The debate continues: we can only note the issues, but cannot enter into the debate here.

Other scientist-theologians have approached the science–religion frontier from the standpoint of biology rather than physics. Arthur Peacocke (1924–2006) was a biological scientist who held academic posts at the universities of Birmingham and Oxford, making a substantial contribution to DNA theory. Peacocke became a reader in the Church of England in 1960, and subsequently gave up his work as an academic scientist, like Polkinghorne, to undergo full ordination as an Anglican priest. Peacocke supports the Darwinian theory of biological evolution, and edited an anthology on the theory, entitled *Evolution: The Disguised Friend of Faith?* Peacocke views the evolutionary processes in the world as God's actions, perceiving God – like Polkinghorne – as setting the initial laws of the universe, but continuously creating the world. The continuous process of evolution requires destruction as well as creation, in order to allow new beings to be born, and he argues that this inevitably involves suffering, in which God himself participates.

Contrary to the impression that is sometimes given by the creationist–evolutionist controversy, the Church is generally favourable to scientific progress, and does not attempt to stop the tide of scientific and technological advance. One of the six Programmes of the World Council of Churches is 'Justice, diakonia and responsibility for creation', which encompasses 'Faith, science and technology', promoting discussion of technological advance and awareness of its ethical implications. In 1970 the Church of Scotland began The Society, Religion and Technology Project, located in Edinburgh with a full-time staff who disseminate information independently of pressure groups, and organize events on topical issues relating to science and religion. Generally, the attitude of the churches is favourable to scientific and technological advance, but Christians typically believe that there are limits to the legitimate use that should be made of such knowledge. The greatest concerns lie in the field of biotechnology, with climatology and nanotechnology also being areas in which responsibility needs to be exercised.

In the field of biotechnology, individual Christians may hold different views on the ethics of stem cell research, cloning and GM crops. Most denominations, however, when such matters are officially debated, have supported the research, perceiving that there are substantial medical gains that can be made; for example, by therapeutic cloning (which must be distinguished from reproductive cloning). The churches have been reluctant to condemn genetically modified (GM) crops, acknowledging their potential advantages in alleviating world hunger. Even the Amish are not opposed to GM crops, since they do not interfere with their low-tech lifestyle, even though they are the result of sophisticated technology. Where genetic research appears to rival the divine creative process, however, the Church is concerned. Most denominations, and in particular the Roman Catholic Church, have opposed research that destroys embryos, genetic engineering (such as 'designer babies'), reproductive cloning, the creation of parthenogenic embryos and animal–human hybrids. Interference with the distinctness of species is often perceived as a violation of the creative principle described in the Book of Genesis, where it is said that God created the various species 'according to their kinds' (Genesis 1:25).

The debates that the scientist-theologians have introduced are no mere ivory-tower intellectual hobbies on the part of the participants. Not only do they break fresh ground in the science-and-religion debate; they also have serious practical implications for Christians as science and technology continue to advance.

Chapter 4

Modern Biblical Interpretation

Before the Renaissance there was little questioning of the authenticity and reliability of scripture. The four Gospels, for example, were viewed as four complementary accounts of the same events. Where they appeared to contradict each other, they were possibly describing more than one similar incident. For example, Mark tells us that, the day after his triumphal entry into Jerusalem, Jesus went to the Temple and drove out the vendors and money-changers (Mark 11:15–17). This happened in the final week of Jesus' ministry. However, John's Gospel places the Cleansing of the Temple much earlier – as one of Jesus' first acts to inaugurate his ministry. The apparent contradiction can be resolved by suggesting that there were two such incidents: this was the position taken by the 'harmonizers' – a number of scholars who attempted to reconstruct the life of Jesus by piecing together the Gospel narratives to form a single harmonious work. One early attempt was by Andreas Osiander, whose *Harmony of the Gospels* does precisely this.

It was generally accepted that the Bible was written by the people who were traditionally identified as its authors. The first five books were written by Moses, who chiselled out the Law on tablets of stone at God's dictation (Exodus 34:1); the Gospel writers were either Jesus' immediate disciples (Matthew and John) or close associates of theirs (Mark and Luke); the letters that bear Paul's name were all written by him; and John's Gospel, his three letters, and the Revelation of John were all written by the same author, who was Jesus' favourite disciple. Renaissance thinkers began to question some of these assumptions. Richard Simon (1638–1712) wrote a work entitled *Histoire critique du Vieux Testament* (A Critical History of the Old Testament) (1678), which noted that the first five books of the Bible (known as the Pentateuch to Christian scholars) contained duplicate passages, and displayed evidence of different styles, thus indicating that these books were the result of multiple authorship, rather than the work of one person – Moses. Succeeding generations, he claimed, had also added embellishments to the narrative. Simon's work was largely ignored until the European Enlightenment, when such issues were re-examined.

Post-Enlightenment scholars distinguish between two types of biblical criticism – 'lower' and 'higher'. 'Lower' criticism aims to establish the correct reading of the Hebrew and Greek texts. The Old Testament was originally written in Hebrew, and the New Testament in Greek. We do not possess any of the original manuscripts, and until the advent of the printing press, scriptures were copied by hand, with parchment and ink. The pages were sewn together and rolled into scrolls, until the 'codex' was invented. A codex resembles present-day books, where pages are bound together inside a cover, making it possible to use both sides of the page. The codex was invented in Pergamum in the third century BCE, and became the preferred format for Christian scriptures around the second century CE. Because the text was copied by scribes, human error was inevitable, and mistakes crept in. More often than not, alterations to the text were accidental, but sometimes a scribe would think he had found an error, and make a change, when in fact the manuscript he was using was authentic.

Textual criticism is a highly specialized area of study. The scholar must not only be conversant with the original languages of the Bible, but know how old an ancient manuscript is. This can be done by carbon-14 dating, but scholars are also able to date manuscripts by examining the evidence about their historical location, and when they are quoted. It is not enough simply to locate the most ancient manuscript, however. It is possible that a very old manuscript is several removes away from the original text, while a younger manuscript is the product of fewer copyings. Equally, one cannot establish the correct text by ascertaining how the majority of manuscripts read: a reliable manuscript may have been copied only once, while an unreliable one might have been used on numerous occasions, thus causing poor texts to outnumber good ones. Textual critics need to know the pedigree of the manuscripts on which they are working – how they have been transmitted, and what their relationship is to the others. It is rather like tracing a family tree. Although there are many textual variants, it is generally possible to establish the correct text and, where there is doubt about a true reading, discrepancies tend only to relate to points of detail. The discovery of the Dead Sea Scrolls was important for textual critics: found in 1947, they include copies of most of the Old Testament, dating from the first century CE – the oldest manuscripts that are known to exist. Many scholars were delighted that the scrolls confirmed their judgements about biblical texts. (Incidentally, the Dead Sea Scrolls do not make any reference to Jesus, contrary to popular belief. They are from a first-century Jewish community, which may or may not have been associated with the Essenes.)

It is important to distinguish the process of scribal copying from the practice of progressively translating the Bible. It is sometimes popularly thought, particularly by those who dislike modern translations, that a modern translation, such as the New International Version, is a rewritten form of the old King James Version (KJV), which used to be regularly used in Protestant churches until the 1960s, or even that it is at second or third remove from the KJV, since a number of translations in modern English were published in the twentieth century. Very few translations are produced without recourse to the original Hebrew and Greek text (or as close to it as we can get). One exception is *The Living Bible* (1965), which was a rewrite based on the American Standard Version (1901), but which is little used in churches.

'Higher Criticism' of the Bible

The Bible poses other questions than how its manuscripts should be read. These can perhaps be best understood by taking a passage that seems superficially unproblematic, but which, on closer examination, opens up a range of quite complex issues. Consider Luke's account of Jesus reading in the synagogue in his home town:

> He went to Nazareth, where he had been brought up, and on the Sabbath day he went into the synagogue, as was his custom. And he stood up to read. The scroll of the prophet Isaiah was handed to him. Unrolling it, he found the place where it is written:
> 'The Spirit of the Lord is on me,
> because he has anointed me
> to preach good news to the poor.
> He has sent me to proclaim freedom for the prisoners
> and recovery of sight for the blind,
> to release the oppressed,

to proclaim the year of the Lord's favour.'
Then he rolled up the scroll, gave it back to the attendant and sat
down. The eyes of everyone in the synagogue were fastened on him,
and he began by saying to them, 'Today this scripture is fulfilled in
your hearing.'

(Luke 4:16–21)

The average believer probably understands the story as a
straightforward account of Jesus reading Jewish prophecy in the local
synagogue, and claiming to be its fulfilment. If one reads on, one
learns that the congregation display pride at the local carpenter turned
preacher, but Jesus goes on to offend them, to the extent that they
attempt to push him off a cliff, thus demonstrating the veracity of
Jesus' statement, that 'no prophet is accepted in his home town' (Luke
4:24).

Biblical scholars cannot be content to let matters rest with this
explanation. Luke is one of four Gospel writers, and one initial
question is therefore whether this story is also recorded by the other
evangelists. We find, in fact, that Matthew and Mark take up the story
of Jesus returning to Nazareth and causing offence, but they do not
record the incident in the synagogue. John's Gospel, which is probably
not reliant on these other Gospels, tends to be different in character,
and does not include the story. The passage purports to describe a
first-century Sabbath synagogue service – but what is happening at it?
Jesus is given the scroll of the prophet Isaiah, which he unrolls. (There
is a textual variant in the Greek at this point: some well-accredited
ancient manuscripts have the word 'opening' instead of 'unrolling'.)
Isaiah belongs to the Prophets (the second main section of Jewish
scripture), not the Law (or Torah – the first five books of the Jewish
scripture): it is normal – at least today – for the main sabbath reading
to be from the Torah. Are we to assume that Jesus is given the second
lesson to read, or was it first-century Jewish practice to read equally
from the Law and the Prophets? Does Jesus choose the passage from
Isaiah, or was there a fixed lectionary that made it the set passage for
the day? Jesus reads the passage and then makes a comment. Was this
normal? Was he acting as the rabbi (the synagogue's teacher)? Jesus
is sometimes referred to as 'rabbi', so it is possible that he was
providing a rabbinical comment on the passage. When Jesus declares
that Isaiah's prophecy is fulfilled, what does he mean? Is he referring
to himself as the fulfilment of prophecy, or might he have intended a
more general message of Jewish deliverance from the Romans?

The passage contains quotation, and the cross-reference must therefore be examined. When we examine the text of Isaiah 61, which Jesus reads, we encounter some problems. First, Luke's quotation is taken directly from the Septuagint, which is the Greek version of the Jewish scriptures, translated in Alexandria during the first three centuries BCE. ('Septuagint' literally means 'seventy', on account of a legend that 70 translators took 70 days to complete it.) Jesus would hardly have been likely to read publicly in Greek – if indeed he could do so – to an Aramaic-speaking congregation. Perhaps, then, Luke is using literary licence here, not thinking it particularly important to record the exact words that Jesus might have read, but using a version of the Bible with which he, Luke, was familiar. Even so, Luke (or Jesus) is not quoting accurately: he inserts an extra line and omits another. Isaiah has, 'He has sent me to bind up the broken-hearted' after the word 'poor' (Isaiah 61:1), and 'to release the oppressed' is not part of this passage, but from another chapter (Isaiah 58:6). What is Luke doing here? In the ancient world, of course, writers would not have personal libraries to consult, and would either have to visit a synagogue to consult its scriptures, gain admission to one of the ancient world's few prestigious libraries, if they were accessible, or work from their personal memory. If Luke is quoting from memory, it is more remarkable that he quotes with such accuracy than that he does not faithfully reproduce the Isaiah passage. All this raises the question of whether Luke is trying to record a real incident in Jesus' ministry, or whether he is using – or even creating – a story, the purpose of which is to define the aim of Jesus' ministry, namely to preach about the kingdom of God to the marginalized people of his time – the poor, the oppressed, the prisoner.

Further light may be shed on the story by asking who Luke was, and here we get into the realms of historical criticism. Luke makes no claim to have been an eye-witness to the events he describes (Luke 1:1–4), although it has sometimes been suggested that he was one of the 70 disciples that Jesus sent out (Luke 10:1–24), or that he was one of the two disciples on the Emmaus Road who encountered Jesus after his resurrection (Luke 24:13–35). A historian, of course, cannot simply accept such claims uncritically: they need careful scrutiny. Hagiography is different from history. Somewhat more certain is the belief that Luke was part of the early Christian community, a physician, one of Paul's travelling companions, and a Gentile. If this last point of detail is correct, it poses a further salient question regarding the synagogue incident. How familiar would Luke be with synagogue worship? While a number of Jewish scholars have welcomed Luke's account as shedding important light on first-century synagogue practice, it must be asked whether, as a Gentile, he would have attended a synagogue service, whether he is merely guessing at what would happen, or whether he was given the story by a reliable (or maybe not so reliable) source.

The above discussion demonstrates how a seemingly simple piece of biblical narrative can raise a hornet's nest of critical questions. It also shows how a variety of types of criticism can be brought to bear on the Bible. There is *source criticism*, which seeks to explore the material on which an author draws. There is *redaction* criticism, which examines how various written sources have been assembled and edited. Related to these is *historical criticism*, in which the historian seeks to establish the truth about the past by critically assessing the source material, some of which may be written, and some circumstantial. *Literary criticism* considers the various genres that are used in scriptural writing and what the text means. Because the Bible was not originally written in English, *linguistic criticism* is needed, to attempt to shed light on original meanings. *Form criticism* is the study of a number of different types of narrative that are employed in the Bible, and it has been thought that the study of different 'forms' could help to determine the historicity of the Gospels in particular. In recent times there has emerged an interest in what is called *reader criticism*. Traditionally, study of the Bible has focused on questions relating to the authorship, the content, the sources and the language. But who would be the primary readership of the biblical literature? If we can ascertain who the intended readers were, this can help us to determine the author's purpose, the context of the work, and its probable interpretation. We shall examine these types of criticism in turn.

Source Criticism and Redaction Criticism

After Richard Simon's observations on Genesis passed unnoticed, Jean Astruc (1684–1766) noted that the book of Genesis uses different names for God. Sometimes God is referred to as Yahweh (or Jahweh), and at other times as Elohim. Astruc suggested that Moses might have used earlier sources, rather than received the Books of the Law as a direct revelation from God. This suggestion was again ignored until John Gottried Eichhorn (1753–1827) noted that the so-called J and E sections were accompanied by other distinctive characteristics. ('J' denotes those sections where the word 'Jahweh' is used, and 'E' denotes the 'Elohim' passages.) The theory was further developed by the German scholars Karl H. Graf (1815–69) and Julius Wellhausen (1844–1918), and has come to be known as the Graf-Wellhausen hypothesis. According to this hypothesis, the J and E sources combined to form a J-E source, which later was combined with at least two other sources: a 'priestly' source (P), whose interest seems to lie in the priesthood and system of sacrificial rites and festivals associated with the Tabernacle, and a later Deuteronomic (D) source, containing legislation that stems from a later date than the previous texts.

The Graf-Wellhausen hypothesis suggested not only that Moses was not the author of the first five books, but that they come from a much later period. Moses is reckoned to have lived around 1230 BCE, while J and E are dated around 1000 BCE (the early days of the Israelite monarchy), with D coming from the seventh century BCE. P is reckoned to have been written after the Babylonian exile, in the sixth century BCE. The document D is connected with a story set in the reign of King Josiah (c. 649–609 BCE). The story goes that while the Jerusalem Temple was being repaired, the high priest Hilkiah discovered a law scroll that apparently had been lost. It was brought to the young king, who was shocked to find that it contained requirements that had been forgotten and gone unobserved. The king ordered a public reading of the book and a period of repentance and restitution. Modern scholars are more inclined to view the story as a myth devised to legitimate a new book. If this book was so important, it is unlikely that it would simply have been mislaid, and the public reading of a text was the recognized method by which a book was admitted to the canon of scripture.

The Synoptic Problem

Although there remain conservative Christians who do not accept the Graf-Wellhausen hypothesis, source criticism relating to the New Testament is more welcome. This is due to the fact that there is a genuine problem to be solved in connection with the clear interdependence of the first three Gospels. There are many overlapping passages among the writers of the three so-called 'synoptic' Gospels. The word 'synoptic' means 'seen together', since it is possible to arrange much of the text of Matthew, Mark and Luke side by side, viewing them together at a glance. Often the text is identical, not merely similar, clearly indicating a literary dependence. The problem of deciding how this overlap occurred, and what the common and distinctive sources for each evangelist are, is known to scholars as 'the synoptic problem'. The problem has exercised the minds of scholars since the late eighteenth century, and much has been written about it.

Just over three-quarters of Mark's material can be found in either Matthew or Luke, with a further 21 per cent found in either one of these two Gospels, leaving only 3 per cent of Mark's material which cannot be found elsewhere. Only one fifth of Matthew's Gospel is unique to Matthew, and 35 per cent of Luke's Gospel unique to Luke. Additionally, there is an overlap of material between Matthew and Luke, which is not found in Mark – amounting to approximately a quarter of each Gospel. The exact nature of the dependence is still contested. Most commonly, Mark is favoured as the earliest of the three Gospels, although historically Roman Catholics have championed Matthew as primordial. It is speculated that Matthew and Luke copied Mark, with the common non-Marcan material being derived from another source, which scholars refer to as 'Q'. ('Q' stands for the German 'Quelle', which simply means 'source'.) Q may or may not be a written document; it is possible that the overlapping material may be from an oral tradition, or it may be several written or oral sources. It consists exclusively of sayings, not narrative. No such written source has ever been discovered, although one scholar claims to have reconstructed Q (Mack, 1993). Additionally, there is material peculiar to each Gospel writer, the source of which is not Q, if it is accepted that Q is a sayings source. A recent complication on the synoptic problem relates to the discovery of the Gospel of Thomas. This exclusively consists of sayings, with examples of overlap with all four Gospels, not merely the synoptics.

Comparing the Gospels enables us to see how the early Church's message may have developed, and how particular evangelists had specific views and interests. To give one example, when a rich young man asks Jesus about how to gain eternal life, he addresses him as 'Good teacher'. Jesus challenges this salutation, saying, 'Why do you call me good? No one is good – except God alone' (Mark 10:17–18). Luke concurs with Mark's account, adding the detail that the man is a ruler (Luke 18:18), but Matthew alters the material more substantially. In his version, the enquirer simply calls Jesus 'teacher', and Jesus replies, 'Why do you ask me about what is good? One there is who is good' (Matthew 19:17). Perhaps we are seeing a climate of growing respect for Jesus, in which Mark is portraying him as human, while Matthew regards Mark's version as tantamount to a denial that Jesus is divine. Of course, such interpretation is speculative, but the example indicates the kind of comparisons that scholars make, and the kinds of conclusion that are drawn.

Form Criticism

The Gospel writers' ability to copy material from each other was facilitated by the fact that the Gospels are not written as pieces of continuous narrative, like novels, but are made up of fragments of material. A fragment is known as a *pericope* (plural *pericopae*), which literally means 'cut around'. The term indicates that the early Christian community 'cut out' small incidents in Jesus' life or sayings of Jesus, which the evangelists pieced together to construct their Gospels. A number of twentieth-century scholars identified different forms which *pericopae* took, and classified them. This approach, which took its rise in Germany, became known as 'form criticism'. It was introduced in Old Testament studies by Hermann Gunkel (1862–1932), and applied to the New Testament by Martin Dibelius (1883–1947) in his *Formsgeschichte des Evangeliums* ('The History of the Gospels' Forms', 1919) and Rudolf Bultmann in his *Die Geschichte der synopticshen Tradition* ('The History of the Synoptic Tradition', 1921).

The form critics used slightly different terminology from each other, but typically they identified the following material. There are, first, 'pronouncement stories' – incidents in which an incident concludes with an aphorism that sums up the story's purpose. When Jesus is challenged about whether taxes should be paid to the Romans, the story ends with Jesus' words, 'Give to Caesar what is Caesar's and to God what is God's' (Mark 12:17). There are also miracle stories, the prime purpose of which is to portray Jesus as a wonder worker. Then, there are 'legends' – tales of the kind typically associated with religious heroes – such as Jesus' baptism (Mark 1:9–11), his overcoming the devil's temptations (Mark 1:12–13), Peter's confession (Mark 8:27–30), and the resurrection stories, among others. Günther Bornkamm (1905–90) prefers to call such stories *Christusgeschichten* ('stories about Christ'), since they were intended to testify to Jesus' messianic status, and the term leaves open the question of their historicity. Jesus' words are classified into parables, and sayings – the latter being pieces of discourse that are not enshrined in story form. Finally, there is the 'passion narrative' – the account of Jesus' final days. Unlike the other *pericopae*, this narrative is more continuous: although it is made up of numerous *pericopae*, it records events on a day-to-day basis, in contrast to the rest of the Gospel material. This may indicate that it is one of the earliest pieces of continuous material collated by the early Church, since it is the most important part of the Christian message, teaching that Jesus died as the messiah.

One of the purposes of form criticism is to examine the context in which these stories and sayings arose. While not denying that they may have originated in real incidents in Jesus' life, the form critics aimed to show that the Gospel narratives were not biographies of Jesus. They are, as Bultmann put it, 'kerygmatic' in intention. *Kerygma* is the Greek for 'proclamation', and Bultmann's point is that they convey the Church's central message. Broadly, the central message is the proclamation of Jesus Christ; however, the early Christians had more specific concerns. For example, the question of whether or not to pay taxes to the Romans was a particular worry for many Jews and Christians, and the story of the tribute money gives a pronouncement on the issue. The form critics used the term *Sitz im Leben* ('life situation') to denote the context in which such stories and sayings may have arisen, contending that such teachings may not go back to Jesus, but were devised with the purpose of offering guidance on salient issues.

Who Wrote the Bible?

The question of whether stories and sayings arose from the life of Jesus or from the early Church raises important questions about the historicity of the Gospel material. If a significant amount of the Gospel narrative originated in the early Church rather than in Jesus himself, then the Gospels were probably not written by eye-witnesses, but by early Christian leaders. Reaching conclusions on the dating of the various pieces of biblical writing is an important issue in adjudicating on their historicity. Examination of the synoptic problem helps to identify the sequence in which the Gospels were compiled. Traditionally, it was assumed that Matthew's Gospel was the first, since Matthew purports to be one of Jesus' 12 disciples, and thus was assumed to be providing eye-witness testimony. Mark was reckoned to be either an eye-witness who followed Jesus around, or else a friend of Peter, who recounted the story of Jesus to him, which he then transcribed. Luke was supposedly a physician and travelling companion of Paul. John's Gospel stands out from the others, being a much more substantially theological work and relating extended discourses of Jesus. John was nonetheless regarded as Jesus' closest disciple, described in the Gospel as 'the disciple whom Jesus loved' (John 13:23). Paul was regarded as the author of all the letters bearing his name, as well as Hebrews, and the letters of James, Peter, John and Jude were written by the bearers of those names. (Jude was thought to be either the disciple Judas – not Judas Iscariot – or Jude the supposed brother of Jesus.) The author of Revelation, who identifies himself as John, was also thought to be the apostle.

This traditional view of biblical authorship is still accepted by many Christian fundamentalists, although it has largely been abandoned by all but a small handful of very conservative scholars. The traditional view suggests that the Gospels were written early in the Church's life, and is largely based on an uncritical acceptance of the early Church Fathers' writings, whose judgements about dating and authorship were generally derived from guesswork or pious legend. The church historian Eusebius (c. 265–c. 340) stated that Matthew's Gospel was written down eight years after Jesus' ascension, making its date around 38 CE, and pre-dating Paul's writings. The latest book was reckoned to be Revelation, dated around 90 CE. Modern scholarship has seriously challenged such dating, although there is no exact consensus on when the various books were compiled. Paul's writings are now generally regarded as pre-dating the Gospels: he may have written as early as 45 CE (the earliest date given for Galatians), but was certainly writing by 50 CE, when he is believed to have penned 1 Thessalonians. Romans was probably his last substantial letter (57–8 CE). Mark commenced his writing after Paul had finished: his Gospel could have been completed by 63 CE, but certainly by 85 CE. One should remember, of course, that he was likely to have used older sources, possibly verbatim.

As well as questions of dating, scholars have questioned traditional views of authorship. None of the Gospel writers identify themselves by name, apart from John, who mentions somewhat cryptically 'the disciple whom Jesus loved', 'This is the disciple who testifies to these things and who wrote them down. We know that his testimony is true' (John 21:24). As Pope Benedict XVI agrees in his *Jesus of Nazareth*

(2007), the connection between the evangelist and the apostle is not explicitly made, and he expresses the view, shared by numerous scholars, that individuals named in the Gospels need not be thought of as single individuals, but as schools of thought whose writings have related, but not necessarily identical, authors. This theory explains the fact that the ideas in John's letters bear a close resemblance to those of John's Gospel, but yet are not wholly consistent with them.

The authenticity of some of Paul's writings has been challenged. The 'pastoral epistles', two written to Timothy and one to Titus, presuppose a community that has become highly institutionalized, with overseers, deacons and elders – a state of development which most scholars believe was highly unlikely only twenty years after Jesus' death. Of the remainder of Paul's letters, Ephesians is fairly consistently rejected as an authentic Pauline piece of writing, principally because of its style, which seems markedly different from his other writings. The authenticity of Colossians and 2 Thessalonians has also been challenged, although there is less agreement about these. Hebrews is consistently rejected as the work of Paul: it has no salutation, and is a piece of neo-Platonic writing, mainly explaining the role of Jesus Christ as the Great High Priest.

The Quest for the Historical Jesus

If the Gospels were not written by eye-witnesses, then to what extent can they be relied on to provide an accurate account of Jesus' life and teaching? These developments in biblical scholarship were accompanied by attempts to reconstruct the life of Jesus in a more sceptical intellectual climate. In all, we can detect three stages in the quest for the historical Jesus: the liberals, who still believed it was possible to construct a fairly continuous biographical account of Jesus' life; the more radical form critics, who sought to find an underlying *kergyma* beneath the layers of myth; and what has become known as 'the third quest', which believes one can obtain a picture of Jesus' essential character and purpose, if not the biographical details. Although most of the contributors to the 'Jesus debate' have been Christians, Jews and non-believers have also made their mark.

The post-Enlightenment attempts to reconstruct a picture of Jesus were influenced by a number of factors. These scholars based their portrayals on reason, rather than faith or tradition, which had thitherto prevailed. Historiography was beginning to take its rise as a science, and the critical methods of the historian became applied to the Bible. No longer could a historian believe in 'special books' that merited special pleading to give their content a privileged status. The rise of science had given rise to scepticism regarding miracles. The laws of nature were uniform, and the Scottish philosopher David Hume (1711–76), in particular, argued forcefully against the possibility of miracles. If a life of Jesus was to have any credibility, then the miraculous components had to be expunged.

The quest for the historical Jesus is generally reckoned to have originated with Hermann Samuel Reimarus (1694–1758). His portrayal of Jesus went against the Church's traditional understanding. Jesus, he claimed, was a political leader, who had messianic delusions. His mission was unsuccessful and, as a face-saving device, his disciples stole his body, claiming that he had been resurrected. Unsurprisingly, Reimarus' views aroused considerable hostility, and they were vigorously criticized by J. S. Semler (1725–91). Semler, however, challenged the traditional views of biblical authorship, and questioned whether the Old and New Testaments had equal authority.

Various scholars in the second half of the nineteenth and the early years of the twentieth century constructed 'lives' that explained away the miraculous components. Miracles were ordinary events that had become embellished, or incidents that the participants misunderstood. Some of the healing miracles were attributable to 'mind cure' – a phenomenon that had aroused interest at that time. It was suggested, for example, that at the Cana wedding (John 2:1–11), Jesus did not really turn water into wine, but had brought along some wine, which he did not produce until the celebrations were well under way. Jesus did not really walk on water, but was seen walking on a log that was floating in the Sea of Galilee. Mark states that women went to Jesus' tomb, where they met a young man 'dressed in a white robe' (maybe an angel) who told them, 'He is risen! He is not here!' (Mark 16:6). One early twentieth-century scholar suggested that 'He is risen!' was a later embellishment, and that the women encountered a guard, who directed them to an adjacent tomb, since they had come to the wrong one (Lake, 1907, p. 262).

Of particular significance is D. F. Strauss (1808–74), who wrote a two-volume *Life of Jesus* (1835–6). Strauss was not altogether satisfied with the approach of rationalizing miracles and explaining healings in terms of 'mind cure'. Commenting on the story of the raising from the dead of Jairus' daughter (Mark 5:21–43), Strauss could not accept the explanation that she was not truly dead, but in a coma. If this were so, he reasoned, Jesus seemed to know of it from afar, and his declared knowledge of her comatose state would have had to be telepathic. Strauss' contribution to the Jesus debate was to introduce the term *mythos* ('myth'), a term that gained enormous importance in the work of subsequent generations of scholars. To call a story 'myth' does not imply its falsehood, but rather that its purpose lies in its significance. In numerous instances, he suggested, the purpose of a Gospel story comes from interests and concerns of the early Church, from whence it originated.

A particularly popular book of this period was *Vie de Jésus* ('Life of Jesus', 1863) by Ernest Renan (1823–92), the first Roman Catholic attempt to compose a life of Jesus. It was based largely on John's Gospel, and was the result of topographical research, capturing the reader's imagination with its vivid descriptions of waving corn fields and Galilean blue skies. It failed to impress Albert Schweitzer (1875–1965), however, who described it as 'Christian art in the worst sense of the term' (Schweitzer, 1910/1963, p. 182). Like the other liberals, Renan rationalized the miracle stories. The raising of Lazarus was a trick carried out with the collusion of Martha and Mary, his sisters. Jesus' life ended with his cry on the cross, 'It is finished', and the resurrection stories take their rise from Mary Magdalene's failure to understand that the garden tomb was only a temporary burial place from which Jesus' body had been moved.

These approaches to the life of Jesus virtually came to an end with Schweitzer, whose *The Quest of the Historical Jesus*, first published in English in 1910, was a survey of the literature in the field, plus his own interpretation of Jesus' life. For Schweitzer, Jesus was an apocalyptist. However, perceiving that a final time of testing (*peirasmos*) was not occurring, Jesus offered himself on the cross as a means of ushering in God's coming kingdom. This did not happen either, and Jesus turned out to be a failure. Schweitzer held that little could be gained from the Jesus of history, but rather, as he wrote: 'Jesus means something to our world because a mighty spiritual force streams forth from Him and flows through our time also. This fact can neither be shaken nor confirmed by any historical discovery. It is the solid foundation of Christianity' (Schweitzer, 1910/1963, p. 397).

Schweitzer's conclusion offers a form of Christianity that is not reliant on the findings of historians, but he leaves the reader with a somewhat vague 'Jesus mysticism', which emanates from, but does not clearly relate to, a first-century failed apocalyptist.

New Approaches to the Historical Jesus

Rudolf Bultmann serves as a good example of a more radical approach to the life of Jesus. In his *Jesus Christ and Mythology* (1960) Bultmann builds his argument on the differences between the worldview that prevailed in Jesus' time, and what 'modern man' is able to believe. Building on the liberal approach that was wary of accepting the miraculous, Bultmann argues that belief in miracles is unacceptable to 'modern man', who organizes his life in accordance with scientific principles. Present-day men and women might claim that they believe in the miraculous, but the very fact that we switch on electric lights and generally use the results of modern science and technology indicates that we have placed our vote in favour of science.

The New Testament worldview is inherently 'mythical'. People believed in a three-decker universe, with heaven above, hell below, and earth in the middle. Supernatural forces were at work on earth: God might intervene to perform miracles from time to time, while Satan could instil evil thoughts in people's minds, or send demons to possess them. In speaking of redemption, the New Testament presupposes a situation where death was the punishment for sin, for which atonement had to be made by a pre-existent divine being assuming the form of a man, who bore the world's sins through crucifixion, rose from the dead, ascended into heaven, and whose return was expected on the clouds of heaven. All this, Bultmann says, is myth, and is no longer acceptable to 'modern man', and must be 'demythologized'.

What we are left with is a picture of a rabbi, who taught 'radical obedience' to God, and who calls men and women to decide to accept newness of life. This radical obedience entails that the Jewish law applies not only to one's actions, but also to one's mind: the distinctiveness of Jesus' teaching is that he advocates cultivating purity of thought, not merely action. In his Sermon on the Mount, he teaches that murder extends beyond physical killing; having feelings of anger in one's thoughts is equally disobedience to the Law of Moses (Matthew 5:21–2). The kingdom of God has arrived at the moment when we decide to accept this newness of life that the 'Christ of faith' offers. Encountering the 'Christ of faith' is not the same a reconstructing the Jesus of history, concerning which we can know relatively little. Accepting Christ's call to decision is something the believer can do now, and to do so is to experience resurrection life. Experiencing this newness of life does not entail belief in the miraculous, but a response in faith to Christ's call.

Bultmann presents a version of the Christian faith that is 'trans-historical'. While the fundamentalist sees importance in accepting the literal historicity of the account the Bible gives of Jesus' life and teaching, Bultmann insists that taking onboard a literal biblical account is both incredible and limiting. However, we are left with very little by way of a historical core of material about Jesus, and Bultmann has been accused of being unduly sceptical in his treatment of the subject-matter. His attempt to separate the Christ of faith from the Jesus of history is problematic. Although one can understand his belief that faith should not be at the mercy of the historian, we must know enough about the historical figure of Jesus in order to identify him with the Christ of faith.

The Third Quest

The 'Third Quest' is the name given to the most recent approaches to reconstruct the historical Jesus. The term was coined in 1992 by N. T. Wright (b. 1948), and the approach is an endeavour to get beyond simply deciding which *pericopae* in the Gospels are likely to be authentic. Can a more holistic picture of Jesus be painted, over and above the fragments? The present-day quest also seeks to place Jesus in the context of the first-century Jewish background from which he comes, and the study of the historical Jesus has been illuminated by the observations of Jewish scholars, most notably Geza Vermes, author of *Jesus the Jew* (1973), the first of several books he wrote on Jesus. Vermes (b. 1924) sees Jesus as a pious Jewish holy man (a *hasid*) who gained a reputation as a miracle worker. The miracle-working aspect of Jesus' ministry receives further emphasis from Morton Smith (1915–91), whose book *Jesus the Magician* (1978) highlights sayings and actions which the author believes are magical formulae and rituals to effect cures; for example, Aramaic expressions like 'talitha koum' and 'ephphatha' (Mark 5:41; 7:34), and the employment of clay made from his saliva to cure a blind man (Mark 8:22–6). The fact that Matthew and Luke do not use these stories, he argues, indicates that Jesus the magician is a primordial theme, which became somewhat suppressed through time.

Other commentators have picked up on different aspects of Jesus, as the Gospels portray him. John P. Meier emphasizes his interest in the marginalized members of society, others have perceived his wise sayings as the key to understanding his personality, while others believe his apocalyptic predictions were his prime concern. Perhaps, again, he was a 'peasant sage', since much of his teaching draws on scenes of farmers planting crops, storing grain and reaping harvests. Tom Wright adopts a somewhat conservative stance in his thesis that Jesus was and is the true messiah that the Jews were expecting.

A number of scholars have recently come together to determine whether some consensus can be reached amidst this lack of consensus. In 1985 Robert Funk (1926–2005) organized the 'Jesus Seminar', whose two hundred members are predominantly from Protestant and Roman Catholic backgrounds, together with a few Jews and some non-believers. No fundamentalists are included. They meet every two years and consider a number of sayings and incidents, then take a vote on their likely authenticity. The Seminar attracted publicity on account of its method of using coloured balls to vote: attendees place coloured balls in a container to indicate their assessment of the likelihood of the incident or saying being authentic: red for 'certain', pink for 'probable', grey for 'possible' and black for 'unlikely'. The Seminar is, of course, controversial. Some have hailed Funk as a 'the most brilliant, the most creative … scholar of our time' (Powell, 1998, p. 76) while others have described the Jesus Seminar as 'an academic disgrace' (Howard Clark Kee, *Los Angeles Times*, 12 March 1991, B6).

Scholarship and the Layperson

The direct impact of these debates on the average believer tends to be minimal, with most Christians accepting an almost literal understanding of the biblical narrative. Academic debates about the nature of Jesus of Nazareth, or academic study of the Bible, tend to be confined to church seminaries. Occasionally, a scholarly publication captures public attention. There is mild interest in the Jesus Seminar, and in the 1960s John A. T. Robinson, then Bishop of Woolwich, aroused much public interest with his *Honest to God*, which disseminated some of the ideas of scholars like Bultmann, Dietrich Bonhoeffer and Paul Tillich. Very occasionally, scholars succeed in popularizing their ideas: one rare example was William Barclay (1907–78), whose Bible commentaries are still read enthusiastically by the laity.

As Bultmann (1958, p. 11) himself acknowledges, faith must be 'more than a walk through a museum of antiquities', but is a 'continuous dialogue with history' in which the believer responds to the demands that the gospel makes. Popular Christian literature about the Bible seeks to promote Bible reading, coupled with prayer, helping the reader to live out its ideas in daily life. The Christian faith requires devotion and obedience, rather than scholarship.

Chapter 5

Mission and Ecumenism

Christianity is very much associated with mission. The word 'mission' is not biblical, and its first use appears to have been by Saint Ignatius of Loyola, who was a soldier turned priest and founder of the Jesuits (a Roman Catholic religious order) in 1540. Christian mission draws on Jesus' parting words to his disciples, as recorded by Matthew: 'Therefore go and make disciples of all nations, baptizing them in the name of the Father and of the Son and of the Holy Spirit' (Matthew 28:19).

Although most scholars believe that this verse is a later addition to Matthew's text, this 'Great Commission' of Jesus remains an imperative for Christians today. The Christian faith was probably the first to aim deliberately at propagating its message to the entire world. This was not practised by the Jews, Persians, Greeks or Romans, whose religions had an impact on their neighbours, but who did not aim to convert the world.

There are several reasons for Christianity's proselytizing character. Initially, the Christian faith began as a Jewish sect, which believed that the promised messiah had come in Jesus of Nazareth. Judaism itself had begun to spread, not through mission, but because followers of the faith had become dispersed throughout the Roman Empire, and had formed their diaspora communities with their synagogues. Paul confesses that, before his conversion, the synagogues were the places at which he hunted down the Christians (Acts 22:17), and on becoming a missionizer himself Paul almost invariably sought out the local synagogue in his travels, in order to preach and debate. The Book of Acts records him as visiting synagogues in Pisidian Antioch (13:14–15), Iconium (14:1), Thessalonica (17:1), Beroea (17:10), Athens (17:16), Corinth (18:1) and Ephesus (18:19). In common with other Jews, Paul and the early Christians had an aversion to 'idols':

these are specifically mentioned in connection with his visits to Athens and Ephesus. The use of physical images to represent the divine, which was characteristic of the Graeco-Roman religions, was perceived as a violation of the second of the Ten Commandments: 'You shall not make for yourself an idol in the form of anything in heaven above or on the earth beneath or in the waters below. You shall not bow down to them or worship them ...' (Exodus 20:4–5).

In more recent times, Protestant missionaries in particular have commented unfavourably on what they perceived as 'idol worship' in Hinduism, Buddhism and various primal religions. God may not be worshipped in physical form.

Although Jews do not actively proselytize, conversion was permitted, and one of the early debates among Christian leaders was whether those who converted to the Christian faith had to reach it through Judaism. The Jews themselves largely disowned Christianity as an expression of their faith, however. This was probably not so much because the Christians preached that the messiah had come, which was a Jewish expectation. More problematic was the fact that Jesus had died without making any significant impact on the physical plight of the Jews under Roman rule, and also that the Christians went on to claim that Jesus was divine. According to Jewish thought, the messiah would be a human figure, although a remarkable one.

Although Judaism tended not to be missionizing, the idea of securing the world's salvation was a Jewish concern. The psalmist writes, 'all the ends of the earth have seen the salvation of God' (Psalm 98:3), and it was expected that God would judge the world, and not merely the Jewish nation (Psalm 98:9). As God's chosen people, the Jews were given the responsibility for saving all nations. God says to Abraham, 'all peoples on earth will be blessed through you' (Genesis 12:3), and it was an expectation that the Jews, by keeping God's covenant, would secure the salvation of 'the peoples' (the Gentiles) as well as their own. The idea of vicarious atonement was embedded in Jewish thought – for example in Isaiah's 'suffering servant', who would be 'a light for the Gentiles' and 'bring my salvation to the ends of the earth' (Isaiah 49:6). However, if, as Paul contended, the Law was replaced by faith in Christ, then a different means of saving the world was needed. Men and women needed to find faith in Jesus Christ, and they could only obtain this if they heard the gospel. Hence the missionary imperative.

'Waves' of Christian Mission

Christianity propagated itself in a number of 'waves'. After the apostolic period, Church Fathers such as Tertullian and Justin Martyr wrote 'apologies' – treatises on behalf of the Christian faith, defending it against common criticisms. ('Apology' literally means 'discourse on behalf of', from the Greek *apo* and *logos*.) As the Roman Empire spread, Christianity moved with it, and received considerable impetus through the Emperor Constantine, who converted to it. Members of monastic orders were instrumental in establishing Celtic versions of Christianity, particularly in Ireland and Scotland.

Of the early Celtic missionaries, Patrick (c. 390–c. 460), Columba (521–97) and Brigid (c. 451–525) are particularly well known among Christians, especially in Britain, although the real facts surrounding their histories are difficult to determine. Saint Patrick was born in Britain and raised as a Christian. At the age of 14 he was captured by Irish raiders, and taken to Ireland as a slave. He escaped back to England, where he received a vision that he should return to Ireland to spread the gospel. Patrick's training for the priesthood appears to have consisted mainly of learning the rule of a religious order, rather than intensive study of the Latin Bible. Patrick was ordained bishop, and he is credited with the baptism of thousands of Irish converts, the conversion of local kings and victory in contests with the rival Druids. It is said that he banished snakes from the island. This is a somewhat dubious claim, since it is doubtful whether there ever were snakes in Ireland, and it has been suggested that 'snakes' was a poetic way of referring to the Druids, or perhaps the Pelagians, to whose heresy Patrick was opposed.

It is hard to be certain of the extent of Saint Patrick's distinctive achievement in Ireland, not only because of the problem of distinguishing between hagiography and history, but because it is evident that Patrick was not the only missionary in Ireland at the time. Pope Celestine I (422–31) sent Palladius to be Ireland's first bishop, possibly to ensure that orthodox doctrine prevailed against the exiled Pelagians, some of whom had found their way to Ireland. Patrick is particularly associated with his explanation of the Trinity, which he compared to a shamrock, having three identical leaves, but remaining one single plant. He is also credited with penning the famous hymn, known as Saint Patrick's Breastplate, which begins, 'I bind unto myself today / The strong name of the Trinity', and continues to be sung by Catholics and Protestants alike, although historians are now generally agreed that the hymn cannot be traced to Patrick. Ireland's patron saint – his saint's day is celebrated on 17 March (the assumed date of his death) – Patrick continues to grow in popularity and is also venerated in the Orthodox tradition. He is believed to be buried in Down Cathedral, Downpatrick, in County Down, Ireland, together with Saint Brigid and Saint Columba.

Saint Columba's work involved the conversion of the Picts, and he gained an audience with King Brude (Bridei). According to the Venerable Bede (c. 673–735), who wrote a history of the Church in England, the king was won over to the Christian faith. As with many saints, some of the stories about Columba are no more than hagiography. Adomnán's *Vita Columbae*, for example, recounts how Columba saved a swimmer who was being pursued by a monster in the River Ness by making the sign of the cross and admonishing the monster with the words, 'You will go no further.' The story may lack authenticity, but – as well as making Columba the first recorded person to see the Loch Ness Monster – it serves to show the regard in which Columba was held, and of course the power attributed to the gospel.

Columba's lasting achievement was the establishment of Iona Abbey. The island's abbey, built in the medieval period, was rebuilt in the twentieth century, and is the home of the ecumenical Iona Community, founded by George MacLeod (1895–1991) in 1938. George MacLeod was minister of Govan Old (Church of Scotland) Parish Church, set in a deprived area of Glasgow. He wanted to break down social barriers, and set up the Iona Community in 1938, using ministers, students and unemployed labourers to rebuild the premises. The Community welcomes pilgrims, who may either make a day visit or else stay for a period, during which they share in the Community's life and worship. The Community is international, with members drawn from Presbyterian, Anglican, Roman Catholic, Lutheran and Quaker traditions.

Mission in Slavic Countries

Despite the fall of the Roman Empire, Christianity continued to thrive, moving north as well as west. Its Roman version remained its principal form, with the Church's liturgy in Latin. However, the Eastern Church, with its centre in Constantinople, encouraged the use of vernacular languages in its worship. From the ninth century onwards Christianity's spread was more determined by political factors than by missionaries directly persuading people to embrace the faith. The mission to the Slavs began when Prince Rotislav of Great Moravia asked the Church at Constantinople to send missionaries. Emperor Michael III and Photius, Patriarch of Constantinople, sent Cyril (Cyrillus, 827–69) and his brother Methodius (c. 825–84). In order to translate the liturgy and parts of the Bible into the Slav language, Cyril devised a new alphabet – Glagolitic – which employed Greek, Armenian and Hebrew characters. (The Cyrillic alphabet is named after Cyril, and is developed from his Glagolitic script. It is still used in Russia and some other Slavic countries.) Because of their use of the vernacular language, Cyril and Methodius were more successful than their German rivals in winning the population to Christianity. However, when the Slavic kingdom became divided between the Germans, the Czechs of Bohemia and the Magyars of Hungary, the Slavic priests were expelled and the Latin liturgy was re-established.

The Slavic priests took refuge in Bulgaria, where it is said that Prince Bogoris was converted to Christianity on seeing a picture of the Last Judgement painted by Methodius. Bogoris was baptized in 863, whereupon he attempted to impose Christianity by force upon his subjects. The Church in Bulgaria never became a national independent Church, but came under the authority of Constantinople. The Church in Bulgaria today is now governed by its own Holy Synod, which is subject to Constantinople's jurisdiction.

Poland experienced an influx of Moravians, and its first missionaries were Slavic. In 965 Princess Dombrowka arrived from Bohemia to marry Duke Mieczyslav. A number of Slav priests accompanied her, and Mieczyslav converted to Christianity the following year. He then demanded that all his subjects should follow his example, ordering the destruction of pagan images and the abolition of rites associated with them. Initially, German priests who favoured the Latin rites worked alongside the Slav ones, but finally the first Polish bishopric, set up at Posen, came under the Archbishop of Magdeburg's authority, thus making Roman Catholicism Poland's official religion.

The Magyars (Hungarians) were surrounded by Christian nations by 950, when the Emperor Otto I insisted on sending Christian missionaries. In 997 King Stephanus, on acceding to the throne, compelled his subjects to undergo baptism. In 1000 the Archbishop of Gran presided over a ceremony in which he received a golden crown from Pope Sylvester II, conferring on him the title 'His

Apostolic Majesty'. Stephanus continued to travel, preaching to the populace, since the German priests and monks in the country did not speak the language. Despite a couple of lapses back to paganism, Hungary remains firmly committed to Christianity in its Roman Catholic form.

Although legend has it that Saint Andrew visited Scythia (part of Eurasia overlapping present-day Russia), Christianity was established in Russia by Grand Duke Vladimir (980–1015), whose wedding in 988 incorporated his baptism, followed by the baptism of the rest of the people. As in Poland, images of Perun, the high god of the Slavic religion, were destroyed. Vladimir is given the title 'Isapostolos' ('equal to an apostle'), indicating his achievement on behalf of the Christian faith. The Eastern Church allowed the use of the Russian language in its scripture and liturgy.

The Crusades

Some mention should be made of the Crusades. They were not missions, of course, and they are not a part of their history of which Christians are proud, but their lack of success against the Muslims helps to explain Christianity's failure to penetrate the Middle East. Historians differ as to which military expeditions count as Crusades, and when the period of the Crusades ended, but it is generally agreed that during the period from 1095 to 1291 there was intense Christian resistance to the expansion of the Muslims into Anatolia (modern Turkey). The Christianized West wanted to establish a land route to Asia, and to see the return of the Holy Land to Christian ownership, with free access for Christians to the holy sites, especially the Church of the Holy Sepulchre – the traditional site of Jesus' crucifixion. These military expeditions were blessed, first by Pope Urban II, and then by successive popes. The pilgrim soldiers took a vow, which the Church enforced, and were given a cloth cross, which they wore during their 'pilgrimages', as the Crusades were called. Participation in a Crusade was believed to be penitential, serving as an 'indulgence' that would secure one's soul a quicker passage through purgatory. Dying on a Crusade was reckoned to be particularly meritorious, causing the soldier to be regarded as a martyr.

In terms of their results, the Crusades were unsuccessful. Most of the participants in the first Crusade died within the first year of service. Although they recaptured Antioch in 1098 and Jerusalem in

1099, Jerusalem fell back into the hands of Saladin in 1187. The Crusaders failed to secure a Christian-controlled route for pilgrims and traders from Constantinople to the Holy Land, most of the Middle East remaining Muslim. The Crusades were not exclusively waged against Muslims, but also against Jews and heretics. Disappointed by their limited success, the Crusaders turned against the East, sacking Constantinople in 1203, thus forfeiting any hopes of reconciliation of the Great Schism of 1054.

Christianity has typically enjoyed little success in converting to its cause those of major faiths. It has fared better, however, in primal societies, whose religions are pre-literate and whose adherents have had no ambition for their faith to permeate the world.

Roman Catholic Missions 1492–1792

A further stage of Christian mission is usually reckoned to have begun in 1492, when Christopher Columbus (c. 1451–1506) 'discovered' America. Without a land route between Europe and Asia, these having been blocked by Muslims, various explorers – mainly from Spain and Portugal – had attempted to find a sea route. Vasco da Gama (c. 1460–1524) had already set sail in quest of a sea route to Asia, and after he reached India via the Cape of Good Hope the Portuguese were able to colonize the African and Indian coasts, bringing their religion with them. Sponsored by the Spanish monarchy, Columbus' declared aims were religious as much as commercial. When he arrived in the Bahamas, for example, he wrote of the indigenous population: 'They ought to make good and skilled servants, for they repeat very quickly whatever we say to them. I think they can very easily be made Christians, for they seem to have no religion.'

Columbus attempted to gain support for a new crusade to recapture Jerusalem, believing that the establishment of Christian rule in the Holy Land would be a prelude to the arrival and defeat of the Antichrist, heralding the world's final judgement. A Franciscan belonging to St Francis of Assisi's Third Order of Penance, Columbus in his later years authored a work entitled *Libro de las profecias* ('The Book of Prophecies') (1501) with the assistance of Gaspar Gorricio, a Carthusian monk. The book was an interpretation of biblical prophecy, together with early and medieval commentaries, and was an attempt to demonstrate Columbus' divinely commissioned role as the bringer of Christianity to the entire world.

During the sixteenth, seventeenth and eighteenth centuries Christianity was transmitted by means of Jesuit, Franciscan and Dominican missions from Spain and Portugal. One modern writer describes these missions as 'far more important than the Reformation which began in 1517' (Burrows; in Bowden, 2005, p. 769). It is sometimes cynically suggested that these missions were a tool of Spanish and Portuguese colonialism, serving to acclimatize the indigenous peoples to the customs of the Christian colonizers. Pope Nicholas V had issued the papal bull *Romanus Pontifex* in 1455 to King Alfonso V of Portugal, authorizing his sovereignty over foreign lands that the Portuguese discovered or conquered. However, there is little doubt that the missionaries sincerely desired to propagate Christianity as the means of salvation to their new audiences. They travelled to Latin America, Africa and Asia, where they reached as far as Vietnam and China. Because they travelled by sea, their early successes were in coastal regions, but, particularly in Latin America, Roman Catholicism percolated inland, resulting in it becoming the dominant religion throughout the Latin American countries. Later Protestant missions in central and north Africa caused Protestantism almost to catch up with Catholicism in terms of its share of the population, and to become particularly prevalent in South Africa, Namibia, Tonga and Swaziland, among other African states. In India, Christians continue to remain a very small minority (around 2 per cent), but with a slightly greater proportion of Roman Catholics. On the west coast, cities such as Goa are predominantly Catholic, with their churches very much in evidence.

The Colonial Period

Christian mission is particularly associated with Christianity's expansion in the nineteenth and the first half of the twentieth centuries. Historians of mission give 1792 as the start date and 1960 as the end of this period. The year 1792 is significant, being the publication date of William Carey's *An Enquiry into the Obligations of Christians to Use Means for the Conversion of the Heathens*. Carey founded the Baptist Missionary Society in the same year, and began his mission in India. This marked the beginning of a proliferation of missionary societies. The London Missionary Society (LMS) (1795) was set up by Congregationalists, Presbyterians, Anglicans and Methodists, and targeted Asia and the South Pacific. David Livingstone, who pioneered missionary work in Africa, worked for the LMS. The Glasgow Missionary Society and the Edinburgh Missionary Society (later the Scottish Missionary Society) were both founded in 1796, working in West Africa, India, the Caribbean and the Caucasus. The Church Missionary Society (1799) was an English missionary society, emanating from the evangelical movement. In 1810 the American Board of Commissioners for Foreign Missions began to focus on Hawaii. The nineteenth century heralded the rise of a proliferation of missionary societies – well over a hundred by the mid-nineteenth century.

The missionaries' concern went beyond converting the indigenous population to the Christian faith: they were concerned for social improvement, and Christian mission is particularly associated with medical work and education. David Livingstone (1813–73) and Albert Schweitzer are particularly renowned for their medical missions, for example. The prime reason for work in health and education was the showing of Christian love, which went beyond the concern to save people's souls. Additionally, missionaries wanted their converts to study the Bible, and hence literacy was a prerequisite, as was Bible translation, which was an important part of missionary activity. Missionaries also found it easier to gain access to foreign countries if they could declare that their work was medical or educational.

The role of women was particularly important in foreign missionary activity. Roman Catholic missionaries were frequently women in religious orders, while in Protestantism they were often the wives of male missionaries. They were able to serve as role models for the indigenous women, showing how Christianity was practised by women, and often they were able to gain access to homes, talking to the female population and spreading the gospel to them. Women were often given the same range of responsibilities as men, including preaching, teaching, and leading prayer groups. J. Hudson Taylor may have expressed the situation slightly unfortunately when he wrote in 1888, 'We are manning our stations with ladies.' Missionary societies, however, did not accept independent women for mission work, despite the status of women in America having risen, largely due to the effects of the American Civil War (1838–65). The war had caused many women to be widowed or less likely to become married, and hence they had to assume responsibilities for running businesses, banks, farms and colleges. In 1861 philanthropist Sarah Platt Doremus (1802–77) founded the non-denominational Women's Union Missionary Society, setting up training colleges for female missionaries, placing them overseas, and encouraging tens of thousands of local churches to support their work financially and by prayer. By 1910 there were 52 women's missionary societies active in America, with 2,000 women missionaries in the field. Women missionaries tended to gain the reputation for being more likely than men to persevere in difficult tasks. For example, the Wycliffe Bible Translators found that teams of single women were more able to complete a translation project than teams of men. At the time of writing, women in mission outnumber men by a ratio of two to one.

Mention should be made of the Student Volunteer Movement (SVL), which was formed in 1886. Dwight L. Moody had organized a YMCA Bible Conference for students at Mount Hermon, Massachusetts, in July 1886. Over 250 students attended this month-long event, in the course of which a number of young men experienced a call to achieve 'the evangelization of the world in this generation'. During the century 1850–1950 some ten thousand volunteers were sent out. James Hudson Taylor (1832–1905) had founded the China Inland Mission, and many of the student volunteers participated in inland missions. This was a particularly dangerous task owing to their susceptibility to tropical diseases, and only one in five of these missionaries survived longer than two years. Many of these early pioneers took their belongings with them in a coffin, realizing the odds against survival. The Student Volunteer Movement lost much of its momentum around the time of the Great War, which caused some of its younger members to doubt the supremacy of the West and the appropriateness of missionizing the rest of the world. In the early 1960s, SVL ceased to be an independent organization.

With the advent of Protestant mission came the need to make the Bible available in a wide variety of languages into which it had not been previously translated. Initially, just parts of the Bible would be translated into a local language; the Gospel of Luke was a favourite starting-point. Bible translation became organized with the founding of the British and Foreign Bible Society in 1804, and the American Bible Society in 1916. The task of Bible translation remains enormous. According to the British and Foreign Bible Society's statistics, there exist 6,912 different languages worldwide. Only 451 of these have a translation of the entire Bible. Of the remainder, 2,479 have part, leaving 4,421 languages without any of the Bible in their literature. Additionally, there is a need to provide for the blind, necessitating Braille and audio versions, and there is the added problem of poor literacy rates in many countries. At first, the Roman Catholic Church was apprehensive about Bible translation work, holding that scripture should not be read privately, without the Church's assistance with interpretation. Today, Roman Catholicism strongly encourages open access to scripture, and the importance of reading it frequently (*Catechism*, 131–3).

By the turn of the twentieth century a number of issues relating to missionary activity needed to be addressed. Of particular concern was the plethora of missionary organizations and the need for coordination of activities among the various Protestant denominations. Now that Christianity had taken root in a large number of foreign countries, questions relating to leadership arose. It no longer seemed appropriate for the churches to continue to operate as missionary societies in foreign countries. Instead, they needed to enable local church leaders to assume responsibility for their congregations and for wider church governance. Allied to the leadership issue was the question of cultural adaptation. Christianity had been presented by (mainly) white missionaries, who had introduced Western architecture and religious practice, such actions subsequently giving rise to the charge that they had been culturally imperialist, even racist. Might there be ways of expressing the Christian faith that were more amenable to the new cultures in which Christianity had arrived? There was also the issue of training new leaders, and how this might be achieved.

Christian Ecumenism

These questions resulted in a large multi-denominational missionary conference, convened by John Raleigh Mott (1865–1955), who was at that time the Chair of the Student Volunteer Movement. Christianity, particularly its Protestant variety, had fragmented into many different sectors. There are at least 30,000 Protestant denominations today, although this estimate includes some very small ones. These divisions, however, caused problems in the mission field. Denominational rivalry was confusing to the indigenous populations, and lack of coordination involved inefficient use of resources. It became obvious that there was a need for churches to work together, and the World Missionary Conference (WMC) was convened in Edinburgh for this purpose in 1910, attracting some 2,000 delegates.

The WMC was not the first major ecumenical project. The latter half of the nineteenth century had seen several ecumenical enterprises, including the Young Men's Christian Association (YMCA), founded in 1844, with the aim of the 'spiritual improvement' of young men, particularly those in trades. The organization provided recreational facilities, together with opportunities for prayer and Bible study. Its sister organization, the Young Women's Christian Association (YWCA) aided the 'temporal, moral and religious welfare' of women, dealing with issues such as domestic violence, homelessness, financial management, and health. (The YWCA no longer regards itself as a Christian organization, however.) The Evangelical Alliance (also known as the World's Evangelical Alliance) originated in England in 1846, with a US branch – the Federal Church Council of America – being established in 1908. Originally set up to oppose the Oxford Movement – a controversial movement among Anglican clergy whose doctrines and liturgy were close to those of Roman Catholicism – the Evangelical Alliance remains active today, mainly aiming to promote Christianity in its more conservative evangelical form.

The WMC's attendees decided that a permanent organization was needed for its work to continue. The International Missionary Council (IMC) – an association of denominational councils – was set up in 1921, followed by the Faith and Order Commission to consider issues relating to doctrine and ministry, and the Life and Work Commission to deal with societal issues. The two Commissions came together in 1948 to form the World Council of Churches (WCC), and in 1961 the IMC was subsumed within the WCC and renamed the Commission on World Mission and Evangelism.

The World Council of Churches was originally set up in Amsterdam, but its Administrative Centre is now in Geneva. It has some 350 affiliated denominations, the majority of which are Protestant, although recently a number of Orthodox Churches have joined. The Roman Catholic Church declined to join, taking the view that there is only one single Church, not churches in the plural. Although officially remaining outside the WCC, however, Catholic delegates have attended conferences and consultations, and even been involved in preparing documents, including the influential *Baptism, Eucharist and Ministry* report of 1983.

The WCC is not a council in the sense of a supervisory body that exercises control over its members or adjudicates on controversies. It coordinates activities of denominations, and promotes the goal of 'visible unity in one faith and one eucharistic fellowship'. 'Visible unity' does not mean persuading the different denominations to merge together into one single unified organization, although there have been some ecumenical successes of this kind. Diversity is less of a problem than the fact that different denominations do not always recognize the validity of each others' sacraments and ministry. For example, the Roman Catholic Church does not permit its members to receive Holy Communion from a Protestant minister, and Protestants are ineligible to receive the bread and wine at a Roman Catholic Mass. Until the twentieth century, the Orthodox Churches did not recognize the baptism of other believers, requiring anyone converting to Orthodoxy to be baptized by an Orthodox priest.

Christian Mission after 1960

The year 1960 is generally identified as the end of missionary activity's heyday, marking the end of the British colonial period. Although Christian missionaries had not converted 'the whole wide world' to faith in the gospel, they had brought Christianity to virtually every country on the globe. Mission could no longer be seen therefore as outreach to foreign people; more as a mission to all peoples, with Christians attempting to persuade those in their own country, even families and friends, of the truth of the Christian faith.

The 1960s also witnessed a substantial increase in the study and teaching of world religions. No longer were their ancient texts studied in the ivory towers of Oxford and Cambridge, but as living faiths, at 'red brick' universities in the United Kingdom, as well as the more ancient institutions. Adherents to 'non-Christian' religions were no longer to be regarded as benighted heathen, but as members of faiths with a historical pedigree, with their own philosophers, theologians and sacred texts, which merited study and, importantly, respect.

As other faiths gained prestige in Western societies, both through academic study and through immigration, some began to question the appropriateness of converting their followers to the Christian faith. Were there not other societal needs that needed to be addressed, for example relief from famine and poverty, liberation from corrupt political systems, peace and reconciliation, and environmental issues? Surely these were concerns of all faiths, not merely Christianity. Espousal of a 'social gospel' tends to be characteristic of liberal Christians, whereas those of Christianity's more conservative evangelical wing believe that such concerns, important as they are, are secondary to 'winning the world for Christ'. The world's problems, they hold, are substantially due to human sin, from which humanity needs to be saved, and this can only be achieved by the full acceptance of the gospel. Organizations like Samaritan's Purse, headed by Franklin Graham, the son of the celebrated world evangelist Billy Graham, offer humanitarian relief to victims of famines, war and natural disaster, but 'with the purpose of sharing God's love through His Son, Jesus Christ'.

Special Missions and Domestic Missions

A number of specialist missions arose to cater for people in particular circumstances. Examples include the Mission to Seafarers, founded as Missions to Seamen in 1856, until the name was made more inclusive in 2000. The idea for such a specialist mission was reportedly born when the young daughter of John Ashley, an Anglican priest, asked her father, as they walked along the cliffs at Clevedon, near Bristol, how the inhabitants of Steep Holm and Flat Holm Islands managed to get to church. Whether or not the story is authentic, it illustrates the Christian commitment to the ideal that everyone, wherever possible, should have access to a Christian community. The Mission was not an attempt at proselytizing, but an endeavour to meet the spiritual and practical needs of seafarers, whose work can be dangerous and lonely, offering places around the world where seafarers of all nationalities and faiths could stay, relax and worship.

Some Christian medical missions are specifically focused, for instance the Leprosy Mission. When the Mission to Lepers in India was founded in 1878 there was no cure for the disease. Founded by Wellesley Bailey, who had seen the work being done in a small leprosy hospital when he was teaching in India some years earlier, the Mission sought to provide treatment, care and shelter, enabling victims of leprosy to minimize discomfort and avoid the need to beg. In the 1970s substantial progress was made in discovering a cure, but there still remain people disfigured and stigmatized by the disease, as well as the task of immunizing new generations against it. The term 'leper', now considered pejorative, was dropped from the Mission's name in 1962, and it is now known as The Leprosy Mission. Sharing the gospel is part of the Mission's work, but the driving motive is compassion.

While Wellesley Bailey was setting up his Mission in India, parallel work was being done in Hawaii by Father Damien, a Belgian Roman Catholic priest. Father Damien elected to live among leprosy victims on the island of Molokai in Hawaii. He worked with victims there for

16 years, from 1873 until 1889, when he finally contracted the illness himself, and died. On 11 October 2009 the Roman Catholic Church canonized him as a saint in recognition of his work.

Christian mission is not merely mission in non-Christian countries. There are many individuals and families in the West who need care and assistance, and who have had no connection with a Christian congregation. Some of the domestic missions have focused on evangelizing, others on social care, and many on both. One of the most visible organizations is the Salvation Army, founded in 1861 as the East London Christian Mission by William and Catherine Booth, both Methodists at the time. Committed to combating homelessness, poverty and alcoholism, the Salvation Army has expended much energy in recent times helping to trace missing persons. The Church Army is an evangelistic arm of the Church of England, founded in 1882, which undertakes evangelical work among the disadvantaged in Britain and Ireland. Many other Christian organizations are engaged either in consciousness-raising or in direct action on a range of social issues, including domestic violence, drug abuse, racism, unemployment, social justice, peace, and many more. Tackling social issues is as much part of Christian mission as preaching the gospel.

Other forms of mission and outreach target children. The Children's Special Service Mission (CSSM), founded in 1867, continues to organize beach missions, where children assemble for short daily children's services while on holiday at the seaside. The missions are non-denominational, although they tend to be run by evangelical Protestants. They organize religious and social events for children, their aim being to teach them about the Christian faith. Claimed benefits include providing a safe environment for children, while enabling parents to have some child-free time to themselves while on holiday. The CSSM is part of the Scripture Union (SU), an interdenominational organization aiming to encourage the study of the Bible. The SU provides notes on daily set Bible readings for children and adults, encouraging regular and systematic Bible study.

The Church endeavours to provide a presence whenever and wherever it is needed, ensuring that people do not have to find a church building to find faith and compassion. The major denominations have a system of chaplaincies. A chaplain is a religious representative – usually, but not necessarily, an ordained priest or minister – who offers spiritual services in a secular institution, such as a hospital, prison, university or college. Chaplaincy usually involves organizing worship and offering spiritual counselling. The presence of industrial chaplains has grown in recent times. Industrial chaplains typically offer their services free of charge to personnel departments of retail, manufacturing and service industries, making themselves available to staff at predetermined times. The chaplain is thus able to provide a Christian service, while the organizations benefit through having the needs of their workforce more fully met, at no additional cost.

The Interfaith Movement

Christianity has moved on from its colonial missionary era. While many Christian missionary organizations still continue the work of propagating the gospel in non-Christian lands, the development of modern travel and communications has decoupled missionary activity from that of the pioneer explorers. As the empire was ending, global migration was increasing, and in the United States and Europe settlers were arriving from Africa and Asia. It was no longer necessary for missionaries to travel abroad to find people who belonged to other faiths; they were now on their own doorstep. Similarly, Christians were no longer seen as bringers of trade, medicine and education. How were they to relate to their new neighbours at home, who subscribed to Islam, Hinduism, Sikhism, and to a lesser degree Buddhism and Jainism?

Early missionaries had spoken in terms of the 'benighted heathen', implying that other faiths were in complete darkness, awaiting the light of the Christian gospel. In the second half of century, some theologians (although by no means a majority) came to question whether such a sharp division could be made, or whether other faiths might contain something of the light of Christ. Instead of the metaphor of light and darkness, some preferred to speak of greater and lesser lights, offering the analogy of the sun and the moon, the former being the full source of light, the latter reflecting the sun's. The analogy suggested that other faiths might reflect at least something of the light of Christ. For example, they incorporated the worship of God, and commended works of charity, good deeds, and a quest for peace and justice: this was hardly total darkness. Would such acts really go unheeded by God?

Various theologians put forward new models to replace the traditional view that 'there is no salvation outside the Church' (*extra ecclesiam nulla salus*). The missionary J. N. Farquhar, in his *The Crown of Hinduism* (1913), attempted to steer a course between claiming that all paths lead to God and that Christianity offers the exclusive means of salvation. His thesis was that Hinduism is an advanced stage on the evolutionary path of religions, awaiting the final completion ('crowning') by Jesus Christ. Thus, he claimed, Christianity is superior, but an important value attaches nonetheless to Hinduism. A later attempt at promoting this theory was by Raymond Pannikar, who described Hinduism as 'a vestibule of Christianity' (in Hick and Hebblethwaite, 1980, p. 140), suggesting that Christ was present in reality, although not doctrinally, in the Hindu faith. A somewhat different attempt, by the Roman Catholic theologian Karl Rahner, was the theory of 'anonymous Christianity'. Jesus' statement, 'No one comes to the Father except through me' (John 14:6), might seem to suggest exclusivism but, Rahner argues, Christ can be present in other faiths, unbeknown to their followers, carrying out his redeeming work. These attempts to place other faiths within God's plan of salvation have been criticized as patronizing, relegating other faiths into second position behind Christianity, which is promoted as the superior religion.

Somewhat less patronizing is the suggestion by John Hick and others that there will be a further opportunity for salvation in an after-death state. If salvation is through Christ alone, then those who have not accepted him will have a further chance after their life on earth. This would enable those of other faiths to obtain salvation, as well as those Christians whose faith or state of purity was insufficient to gain direct entry into the kingdom of heaven. Hick suggests that this may be the vast majority of humans, Christian and non-Christian. It is not one's religion, he argues, but God through Christ who undertakes the task of redeeming humanity. Hick suggests that this is a kind of Copernican leap, from regarding Christianity as the pivotal point from which salvation occurs, to God himself, who is shared by many faiths.

Whatever theology of world religions Christians subscribe to, the plural societies that emerged in Western countries in the second half of the twentieth century pointed to the need for dialogue rather than forceful proselytizing. Pope Paul VI, in his Vatican II Declaration on the Relation of the Church to Non-Christian Religions, *Nostra Aetate* ('In Our Age', 1965), wrote:

> The Catholic Church rejects nothing that is true and holy in these religions. She regards with sincere reverence those ways of conduct and of life, those precepts and teachings which, though differing in many aspects from the ones she holds and sets forth, nonetheless

often reflect a ray of that Truth which enlightens all men. Indeed, she proclaims, and ever must proclaim Christ "the way, the truth, and the life" (John 14:6), in whom men may find the fullness of religious life, in whom God has reconciled all things to Himself.

The Pope went on to recommend that Christians cooperate with members of other faiths in discussion and collaborative efforts.

During the late 1970s, various local interfaith groups started to form, mainly with the purpose of getting to know members of other faiths, to learn about them through direct encounter rather than merely reading textbooks, and to work together on common concerns, such as the combating of racial and religious prejudice. Such groups are not intended to provide forums for evangelism, or to produce some new ecumenical syncretistic world religion. At national levels, the Temple of Understanding was founded in the United States in 1960, and the Interfaith Network for the United Kingdom in 1987. Both are umbrella organizations, coordinating interfaith work nationally and internationally.

The interfaith movement remains controversial. Most Christians would agree on the value of gaining acquaintance with members of other faiths. Some believe that Christians can actively learn from these other religions, perhaps reclaiming neglected parts of their own tradition, such as meditation. Others fear that there is a risk of putting all religions on a par, suggesting that they have equal validity, or even that they are all teaching the same thing. Many evangelical Christians continue to believe that Christianity teaches the sole truth and means of salvation, and that the only proper interfaith work is evangelism.

Chapter 6

Ethics

We noted earlier, in chapter 2, Augustine's observation that Christians who belong to God's 'heavenly city' are often indistinguishable from those of the 'earthly city', and that only God knows who are true members of the Church. The Christian ethic is deliberately an unobtrusive ethic. There are no 'special obligations' accepted by all Christians. Members of some Christian communities have set themselves apart from the world and taken vows of poverty, prayer, fasting and celibacy, but most Christians live in the world, taking part in family life and work. Some communities have imposed tithing on their members (donating a tenth of their income), but more commonly churches do not impose financial requirements, but recommend that people give as they are able, and in a spirit of generosity. There are no food laws: some Christian communities (such as the Brethren and certain of the Scottish Free Churches) disallow the consumption of alcohol, but others, such as the Benedictines, rely on its sale for their livelihood. Adventists continue to follow Jewish dietary laws, and Roman Catholic monastic orders, such as the Carthusians and Cistercians, are strictly vegetarian, but such restrictions are not observed by Christians more widely. Some Christians smoke and gamble, while others would express strong disapproval at such practices.

The idea of an unobtrusive ethic is embedded in Jesus' teaching. His followers should not be ostentatious in piety, for example. Rather, they should be like salt (Matthew 5:13) – making a difference in the world just as salt enhances food. The Christian is in the world, but not 'of the world' (John 17:16). Although Christian ethics may not seem particularly different from secular ethics, any religious ethic typically adds other features that help the moral life of the follower. The Bible provides stories to inspire the spiritual and moral life, and

Jesus' parables in particular provide concrete illustrations of how to put Christian love into operation. Christians might be less motivated to love their enemies if it were not for the famous story of the Good Samaritan, who stopped to aid the wounded traveller, who was a Jew. Many Christians find help through prayer, or through the sacraments: one function of receiving the body and blood of Christ at the Eucharist is that these signify Christ living within oneself, and directing one's behaviour. Again, belonging to a Christian community affords mutual encouragement, and an organized body of people can achieve much more than isolated individuals. Organizations like Christian Aid, CAFOD (Catholic Agency for Overseas Development), Life, and Christian CND, are able to act corporately, where individuals' impact on issues like the relief of poverty, respect for the unborn child or nuclear disarmament would be slight.

This idea links to other aspects of Christian doctrine that have already been mentioned. Since God's creation is both real and good, there is no necessity to escape from it. Through Adam and Eve's fall in the Garden of Eden, humanity became corrupted, tainted with original sin. Although words like 'sin' are not common parlance among Christians today, sin is nonetheless a central theological concept. 'Sin' must be distinguished from 'sins'. 'Original sin' does not name humanity's first misdeed – a common misunderstanding. It is a condition, not an action, and it is the state that every human is born with. It is transmitted through one's parents, and Augustine held that it enters one's body at the moment of conception. Whether one takes literally the Garden of Eden story or the details of Augustine's theology, Christian teaching is that sin is a deeply embedded human condition, to which everyone is subject. The condition of original sin anticipates any sins (particular misdeeds) that a human being goes on to commit.

Characteristically, religions identify root causes of the human condition, rather than merely offer piecemeal guidance on areas in which life might be improved. Radical reappraisal of one's life is needed, and Christian preaching emphasizes repentance. The earliest recorded teaching of Jesus is, 'The kingdom of God is near. Repent and believe the good news!' (Mark 1:15). This message is reiterated in Peter's speech at Pentecost to the crowd at Jerusalem: 'Repent and be baptized, every one of you, in the name of Jesus Christ for the forgiveness of sins. And you will receive the gift of the Holy Spirit' (Acts 2:38). The literal meaning of *metanoia* (translated as 'repentance') is 'change of mind', indicating that one's underlying thinking needs to change, and that one needs to turn back, or turn around. This idea harks back to a recurring theme in the Old Testament, in which God's people are compared to rebels who must return to their rightful ruler, or to an unfaithful wife who should come back to her husband. (The analogy is of a wife returning rather than a husband, since God is typically assigned the masculine gender.) Just as Adam and Eve succumbed to the serpent's temptation to eat from the forbidden tree, so the Christian is commissioned to renounce Satan and follow Christ.

The Gospel writers associate repentance with baptism, the renunciation of Satan and the receiving of the Holy Spirit. In the story of Jesus' baptism, John the Baptist had been preaching about the need for repentance, and Jesus, on being baptized, experienced the Holy Spirit descending on him. He subsequently withdrew to the desert, where Satan tempted him for forty days and nights. In the Church of England's baptismal liturgy, candidates for baptism (or their parents, when children are being baptized) are asked the following, and answer accordingly.

> Do you reject the devil and all rebellion against God?
> *I reject them.*
> Do you renounce the deceit and corruption of evil?
> *I renounce them.*
> Do you repent of the sins that separate us from God and neighbour?
> *I repent of them.*
> Do you turn to Christ as Saviour?
> *I turn to Christ.*
> Do you submit to Christ as Lord?
> *I submit to Christ.*
> Do you come to Christ, the way, the truth and the life?
> *I come to Christ.*
>
> (*Common Worship*: 353)

Paul associates the imagery of baptism with death and resurrection. One's old life dies, and one's new life commences. 'We were therefore buried with him through baptism into death in order that, just as Christ was raised from the dead through the glory of the Father, we too may live a new life' (Romans 6:4).

Paul is thinking of baptism by immersion, where the candidate descends into the water, as a dead body is lowered into a tomb. The emergence from the baptismal water is like a resurrection, compared by Paul to Christ's, which signifies the newness of life offered to the Christian. Traditionally, the cleansing function of water (whether baptism is done by immersion or sprinkling) connotes the washing away of original sin. Most Christians regard the rite as symbolic, rather than having any kind of quasi-magical efficacy.

Good Works and Salvation

Christian teaching, then, is that one must get at the root of sin, through repentance. However, the seriousness of sin makes it insufficient simply to do good deeds instead of evil ones. Paul argues forcefully that freedom from the Jewish law entails that salvation is not be gained through works, but rather through divine grace. It is not through one's own merits that salvation is attained. The letter to the Ephesians says: 'For it is by grace you have been saved, through faith – and this not from yourselves, it is the gift of God – not by works, so that no one can boast' (Ephesians 2:8–9).

Faith rather than works has formed part of Christian teaching universally, but it came to be especially emphasized in the Protestant tradition. Protestantism, particularly under the influence of John Calvin, accepted that since salvation is by God's grace (meaning undeserved favour), then only God can bring people to salvation. This led Calvin to embrace the doctrine of predestination: the idea that, at the moment of creation, God, being all-knowing and all-powerful, knows in advance who will turn to Christ and who will not. The former are called 'the elect' and the latter 'the damned'. This may seem unfair, but it is a logical consequence of holding that salvation is not through one's own efforts, and Calvin emphasized that one cannot fully understand God's ways.

If one is sinful, then everything one does stems from a state of sin – good works as well as evil ones. The *Westminster Confession of Faith* (1647), whose authors were strongly influenced by Calvinism, states that:

> Works done by unregenerate men ... because they proceed not from an heart purified by faith ... are therefore sinful, and cannot please God, or make a man meet to receive grace from God. And yet their neglect of them is more sinful, and displeasing to God. (*Westminster Confession*, XVI, vii)

The Roman Catholic position rejects the idea that a loving God would predestine anyone to eternal damnation. Such a state is the fate only of those who wilfully turn away from God and remain in that state, unrepentant (*Catechism*, 1037). Although some Protestant denominations are firmly committed to Calvinism, such as the Southern Baptist Convention, it is important to recognize that not all Protestants, by any means, would subscribe to Calvin's doctrine of 'double predestination'. Rank-and-file believers would certainly agree that God's grace is necessary in the salvation process and that good works are insufficient, but would profess ignorance of the precise way in which God's grace works. This is a matter for theologians to discuss.

However divine grace operates, God calls the believer out, marking him or her as separate from the world. This is what is meant by 'holiness', although most Christians would be reluctant to describe themselves as holy. As a theological concept, however, holiness is important in explaining the Christian's relationship with God, and the behaviour that is expected of them. The first letter of Peter reads: 'But you are a chosen people, a royal priesthood, a holy nation, a people belonging to God, that you may declare the praises of him who called you out of darkness into his wonderful light' (1 Peter 2:9).

In practice, the word 'holy' tends to be reserved for God himself, and for especially sacred objects and rites: Holy Bible, Holy Communion, holy water, holy orders. However, the theological purpose of describing God's people as 'holy' is that they are set apart from the rest of world. Being set apart is the basic meaning of holiness, and God's people are called to a life of purity. Paul teaches that one's body should be a 'living sacrifice' (Romans 12:1). In the Jewish sacrificial system, the animals and birds that were sacrificed were set apart from all other possible human use, and they were required to be without blemish. Christian ethics, therefore, acknowledges that one's mind and body are not one's own, but belong to God. When the Bible and the ancient creeds refer to 'the saints' or 'the communion of saints', this is not a reference to spiritual virtuosos who have led lives of supererogatory virtue and thus achieved canonization by the Church. Paul frequently addressed his letters to those 'called to be saints' (e.g., Romans 1:7), meaning those who belong to the Christian community and who can expect to be part of Christ's kingdom when it is realized.

The Christian is not exempt from exhibiting saintly behaviour, however. In his Sermon on the Mount, Jesus instructs his hearers, 'Be perfect, therefore, as your heavenly Father is perfect' (Matthew 5:48). This statement acknowledges the moral quality of the divine: God is the source of goodness as well as of existence. Orthodox thought particularly emphasizes *theosis* – becoming divine – and sees the Christian life as a quest for perfection, given that God is perfect. The Protestant tradition has stressed the notion of 'sanctification' in this regard: repentance and conversion do not make the believer instantly holy or perfect, but the Holy Spirit works as the life force inspiring the believer and providing the cleansing that is necessary for spiritual striving.

Practical Ethics

The three main traditions have slightly different emphases in the way morality is contextualized. We have already noted the Orthodox notion of morality as part of the process of *theosis*: to act rightly is to participate in the divine life. Roman Catholicism continues to be influenced by the work of St Thomas Aquinas, who viewed the moral life in terms of love of God and friendship with him. Protestants have tended to use analogies that recognize God's sovereignty, partly because the concept is biblical, and also no doubt because Protestantism has been associated with nation-states. Protestantism emphasizes the will of God and the glory of God in its moral thinking: 'So whether you eat or drink or whatever you do, do it all for the glory of God' (1 Corinthians 10:31).

In a previous chapter we noted differences in the sources of authority on which each tradition draws. All acknowledge Christ as the supreme source of authority, the Bible, conscience, and – for Roman Catholicism and Orthodoxy – tradition. Christianity acknowledges the authority of both the Old and the New Testaments, and this raises the question of how Christians view the relationship between the two, and why, if both are authoritative, the ethical injunctions of the Old Testament are not completely taken on board by Christians. Should they not be stoning blasphemers and sabbath breakers, draining the blood from animals before eating them, and calling a priest if they find mildew in their home, as the Old Testament instructs (Leviticus 24:16; Numbers 15:32–6; Leviticus 7:26; 14:34–53)? A few Christian fundamentalist groups, such as Christian Voice, claim to accept the whole of the old covenant as well as the new, although they have not gone so far as to accept such obligations.

Fundamentalists tend to regard the Old Testament as a true record of God's dealings with his people, and accept that such commandments were God-given. They may have been valid for that time and place, but they are no longer binding on the Christian.

As a rule of thumb, the Old Testament Law is held to have been superseded by the gospel, apart from requirements reiterated by Jesus or the authors of the New Testament. The Ten Commandments are therefore a prime Christian obligation. Jesus alluded to them when a rich young man asked what he must do to gain eternal life (Matthew19:16–19), and it would be very surprising to find a Christian who was unaware of them. In summary, the Ten Commandments are:

(1)   You shall have no other gods before me.
(2)   You shall not worship idols.
(3)   You shall not take God's name in vain.
(4)   Keep the Sabbath day holy.
(5)   Respect your parents.
(6)   Do not murder.
(7)   Do not commit adultery.
(8)   Do not steal.
(9)   Do not bear false witness.
(10) Do not covet your neighbour's wife or belongings.

                    (Exodus 20:1–17; Deuteronomy 5:6–21)

The above uses the Orthodox and Protestant numbering. Roman Catholicism combines the first and second commandments, separates the two elements of the tenth, and renumbers accordingly.

When asked what the greatest commandment was, Jesus identified two key requirements: 'Love the Lord your God with all your heart and with all your soul and with all your mind', and 'Love your neighbour as yourself' (Matthew 22:37–9). These, he claimed, were not only the greatest commandments, but serve as a summary of the entire Jewish legal system. The principle of loving one's neighbour as oneself, often called 'the golden rule' or the principle of reciprocity, is common to many other religious and secular moral systems, underlining the point that Christianity does not require a special ethic. It is more important to observe principles that are shared in common with other traditions than to devise a distinctive moral code that differentiates Christians from others.

The Concept of 'Love'

The concept of love, which is central to Christian ethics, needs some comment. As one writer has remarked, 'If one were to sum up the practice of the Christian religion in a single word, that word might be "love"' (Catherine Williams, in Bowden, 2005, p. 714). Popularly the word 'love' has connotations of sexual attraction, sentimental devotion to someone, or even infatuation or lust. Christian love relates to the Jewish and Christian concepts of God. God's love for his people is a perennial theme in the Old Testament, where it is often portrayed as analogous to the love of a husband for his wife. The analogy has several important dimensions. Divine love is selective: God has singled out the people of Israel as the special chosen object of his love, according to Jewish thought. Divine love requires commitment, as in a matrimonial relationship, where there are mutual obligations binding on both partners. Love also demands loyalty: the betrothed (Christ and the Church) are nonetheless in a special relationship of devotion and commitment.

God and love are closely associated, to the extent that John asserts that 'God is love' (1 John 4:8). For the Christian, love is bound up with the nature of God. Conceiving of God as a Trinity of Father, Son and Holy Spirit points to a 'social relationship' within the deity. Christian theology conceives of God not as an unmoved mover, or a self-existent self-sufficient being. Love requires someone to love and someone to be loved, and thus God is conceived as a Trinity in which the Father loves the Son (John 15:9), and the believer's love of Christ is reciprocated in being loved by the Father and the Son (John 14:21). Christ's loving relationship with the world is demonstrated by the laying down of his life for his disciples (John 15:13). The centrality of love thus links with the doctrine of the Incarnation, which is held to demonstrate God's love for the world. The most famous biblical verse, familiar to all Christians, is John 3:16: 'For God so loved the world that he gave his one and only Son, that whoever believes in him shall not perish but have eternal life.'

Although the Bible compares the Christian's relationship with God to that of a marriage, the Christian obligation to 'love one another' is not construed in the same sense as carnal love. In his spiritual classic *The Four Loves*, C. S. Lewis distinguishes between four types of love that are mentioned in the Bible. The Greek word *storgē* might be translated as 'affection', and is used to describe relationships between family members, which involve commitment and sometimes sacrifice.

Second, there is *philia*, which is sometimes described as 'Platonic love' and is the kind of relationship that exists between friends. Unlike with our family members, we choose our friends, losing and gaining them as circumstances change. Third, *eros* denotes sexual or romantic love, or even lust. It is a feeling, and can sometimes be uncontrollable: we speak, for example, of 'falling in love', indicating that it can be something that happens to us rather than an emotion over which we have control. The fourth concept, *agapē*, describes the kind of love that is required in the command to love one another. This type of love is sometimes described as a lifestyle, rather than an emotion. It involves the cultivation of a number of virtues, several of which Paul enumerates in a well-known passage in 1 Corinthians – a passage that is frequently read at Christian weddings and funerals, since it sums up the ideal Christian lifestyle. Love is patient, kind, not boastful, courteous, selfless, not easily provoked, does not harbour grudges, seeks the truth rather than spreads malicious gossip, protects and trusts others, and displays hope and perseverance (1 Corinthians 13:4–7). Paul agrees that, of the three principal Christian virtues – faith, hope and love – it is love that is the greatest (1 Corinthians 13:13).

The objects of love are God and one's neighbour. Jesus' most famous explanation of the meaning of 'neighbour' is enshrined in the parable of the Good Samaritan, in which Jesus describes how two Jewish Temple officials ignore a wounded traveller on the Jerusalem–Jericho road, but a Samaritan – a much-despised foreigner – binds his wounds and pays for his keep at a nearby inn (Luke 10:25–37). The story is prompted by a lawyer's question about how one might gain eternal life, to which Jesus replies by citing the commandments about love for God and one's neighbour. This in turn prompts the question, 'Who is my neighbour?' – the answer to which one might have expected a legal expert to have known well. Jesus' conclusion to the parable does not offer a formal definition, but rather poses the question in a different way: 'Which of these three do you think was a neighbour to the man who fell into the hands of robbers?' (Luke 10:36). Jesus' point is that a neighbour is not someone who is defined either ethnically or geographically, but rather anyone with whom a caring relationship is possible.

The story of the Good Samaritan also draws attention to Jesus' ministry to the marginalized in society. Jesus offers teaching, healing and fellowship to women, Gentiles, tax collectors, prostitutes, leprosy victims, and those believed to be possessed by demons. Even on the cross, he offers forgiveness and entry to God's kingdom to a dying robber. In the Magnificat (Luke 1:46–55) – the song of Mary when Jesus' birth is foretold, and which is frequently sung or recited in Christian liturgy – we read of God overthrowing the proud, the mighty and rich, and exalting the humble and satisfying the hungry. Jesus begins his Sermon on the Mount, which most Christians would identify as an important source of Christian moral teaching, with the Beatitudes (a collection of 'blessings' – the word derives from the Latin *beatus*, meaning 'happy'). These single out the disadvantaged and virtuous as the just inheritors of the kingdom of heaven: the despondent, the mourners, the hungry, the meek, the merciful, the pure, the peacemakers and victims of persecution for the sake of Christ (Matthew 5:3–12).

The Sermon on the Mount

The Sermon on the Mount, which has just been mentioned, is a highly important source of moral teaching for the Christian. Matthew implies that Jesus preached it as an extended sermon delivered on a hillside, now called the Mount of the Beatitudes, near Tiberias. The sermon occupies three entire chapters of Matthew's Gospel, and it is more likely that it is a collation of various sayings attributed to Jesus and delivered on numerous occasions. Pope Benedict XVI, in his *Jesus of Nazareth* (2007), suggests that the Gospel writer located the scene on a mountain so as to parallel Jesus with Moses, who received the Law on Mount Sinai. Jesus, indeed, appears to claim for himself a degree of authority equivalent to that of Moses, continually referring to elements of the Law, and adding, 'But I tell you …' Jesus does not, however, recommend that any part of the Mosaic law should be abandoned: in each case he offers an amplification that raises the standard required for complete obedience. The prohibition on murder entails restraining one's anger. 'You shall not commit adultery' implies that one must avoid lustful thoughts. Instead of keeping oaths one has made, it is preferable to avoid making them at all. Instead of requiring an 'eye for eye and tooth for tooth' we should turn the other cheek. Jesus' hearers should love their enemies, not merely their friends or neighbours.

The Sermon on the Mount's demands have caused Christians to ask whether they are meant to be taken literally, or applied in all situations. Is it possible, or indeed desirable, always to turn the other cheek when one is harmed? When Jesus said, 'Do not judge' (Matthew 7:1), was he really implying that one should never criticize, or that his followers should be undiscriminating? Throughout the centuries Christians have offered different suggestions about how Jesus' words should be understood. Some have taken Jesus literally, and tried to achieve the high moral standards that he appears to demand. The Amish, Mennonites and Hutterites have formed their own communities, limiting contact with outsiders and thus reducing the circumstances in which anger, revenge and lack of love might be temptations. Others have suggested that the text of the Sermon has been altered in the process of copying, and that, for example, the exception of adultery in Jesus' prohibition on divorce was abandoned at an early stage (Matthew includes it, but Luke does not: see Matthew 5:31; Luke 16:8). Supporters of New Covenant theology – the view that God has established a new covenant with Christ's followers, which supersedes the old – affirm that Christ's requirements are to be taken literally. However, they acknowledge that it is not possible to attain the standards of perfection that Christ enjoined, and that the sheer impossibility of his ethic illustrates the need for the gospel, with its message of divine grace and the impossibility of attaining salvation through works.

Other views that involve taking Jesus' teaching literally include Albert Schweitzer's idea that Jesus was advocating an 'interim ethic'. Because Jesus expected an imminent apocalypse, he encouraged intensely heightened standards of behaviour in preparation for the coming kingdom. This suggestion has gained little support, particularly since Schweitzer's account of the historical Jesus proved unpopular. However, other Christians, influenced by J. N. Darby (1800–82) of the Plymouth Brethren, have suggested a 'dispensationalist' theory of human history, dividing it into a number of identifiable periods: the age of law, the gospel age, and the coming period of Christ's kingdom. A heightened standard of ethic is required in our present time in order to herald the coming new dispensation.

Still other Christian positions view the Sermon on the Mount as hyperbole, or as illustrating the type of deed that love may sometimes require. It seems clear that no Christian would take Jesus literally when he says, 'If your right eye causes you to sin, gouge it out and throw it away' (Matthew 5:29). In his controversial *Honest to God*, J. A. T. Robinson rejects the view that Jesus was presenting a new Law to his early followers. Rather, he suggests:

The moral precepts of Jesus are not intended to be understood legalistically, as prescribing what all Christians must do, whatever the circumstances, and pronouncing certain courses of action universally right and others universally wrong. They are not legislation laying down what love always demands of every one: they are illustrations of what love may at any moment require of anyone. (Robinson, 1963, pp. 110–11)

They are, as Robinson puts it, 'flashlight pictures of the uncompromising demand which the Kingdom must make upon any who would respond to it'. In other words, if one's problem is the love of money, one might have to forfeit it unconditionally for the sake of God's kingdom, but this is not necessarily an expectation for everyone.

Conscience

In addition to the Church's tradition and the Bible, all three traditions recognize conscience as a source of authority and a guide to moral behaviour. Writing about the Gentiles, Paul says that 'the requirements of the law are written on their hearts, their consciences also bearing witness' (Romans 2:15). Being an inner voice, conscience may seem a somewhat subjective criterion for deciding what is right and wrong, particularly if one thinks of one's 'reactive conscience', which can 'prick' a person with feelings of guilt and remorse. Conscience is not 'gut feeling', however; it also involves reason. Martin Luther wrote, 'As the mind judges, so the conscience dictates' (quoted in Hoose, 1999, p. 11). Conscience literally means 'knowledge with' (from the Latin *conscientia*, being compounded from *con*, 'with', and *scientia*, 'knowledge'), and thus one's personal judgements about right and wrong should be formed in conjunction with one's reason (for example, making inferences from wider principles), with the other sources of authority (scripture and tradition), and with intimacy with God himself. The Second Vatican Council's document *Gaudium et Spes* ('Joy and Hope', 1965) says, 'Conscience is the most secret core and sanctuary of a man. There he is alone with God, Whose voice echoes in his depths.'

Conscience can be unreliable, however, if it is insufficiently trained, or if it has been dulled through repeated misdeeds. In Orthodox thought, *syneidēsis* (the Greek equivalent of *conscientia*) is construed as being in communion with the Trinity, and thus making progress in the acquisition of the divine nature. Understanding and purifying oneself is important to the cultivation of *syneidēsis*, and herein lies the importance of seeking forgiveness for sin of which one is unaware.

Christian Lifestyle and Ethical Issues

For the majority of Christians their life involves a conventional lifestyle, following the customs of the society in which they live, gaining employment, and entering into marriage and family life. These are not requirements, and entry into religious orders is an alternative in some forms of Christianity. Different traditions have different positions regarding holy orders. In the Protestant churches, monasticism is entirely disapproved of, and members of the clergy may marry and have families. Roman Catholicism, Orthodoxy and (to a lesser extent) Anglicanism have monastic orders, with Roman Catholicism having nuns as well as monks. Catholic Clergy must be celibate, while the marriage of clergy is permitted in the other traditions. Whichever lifestyle is followed, Christianity tends to be practised in community and congregational life. As with monasticism, Protestants tend to disapprove of the hermetic life, although both Catholicism and Orthodoxy perceive a role for it: the hermit is able to follow a simple lifestyle, untainted by ambition or greed, and to devote his or her life to contemplation of God.

Christian moral teaching is popularly associated with sexual morality, no doubt because issues such as chastity, contraception, abortion and homosexuality are frequently discussed. Christian moral teaching in fact covers a wide range of activities: obedience to civil authorities, employment and industrial relations, wealth and poverty, war and peace, honesty and truth telling, the media, and crime and punishment, to name but a few. Roman Catholicism and Orthodoxy, being hierarchical in their organization, tend to adopt authoritative positions on moral issues, seeking to make these binding on their members – although this is not to say that members will heed the Church's teaching. Compliance with the Roman Catholic stance on contraception, for example, is very low. Protestants tend to debate moral matters, often in church courts or assemblies, and pass motions, which might be used to influence government policy on a topical matter. The onus in on individual members to reach their personal decisions on controversial matters, based on their understanding of scripture and on their consciences. It is very rare for a rank-and-file member of any tradition to be disciplined for acting contrary to the Church's position. All branches of the Church remain influenced by Augustine's teaching that the distinction between the true heavenly citizens and those who simply belong to the 'earthly city' is not humanly visible. The Church continues to offer salvation and opportunities to mend one's ways. In the Roman Catholic, Orthodox, and some parts of the Anglican traditions, confession and counselling are formally offered, and in all traditions advice can be sought from the clergy or lay leaders.

Regarding lifestyle, Christianity has no objection to the creation of wealth. It is not a sin to be rich, or to demand interest ('usury') on monies that are lent. However, Christians are expected to earn their living honestly: this is normally through one's labour, and some Christians have viewed work as punishment for sin, originally inflicted on Adam for his disobedience. God tells him, 'By the sweat of your brow you will eat your food' (Genesis 3:19). Some Protestants have interpreted this to mean that one should *only* earn one's living through work, and taken this as a prohibition on gambling, where wealth is created through luck rather than effort. Most Christians see no harm in games of chance, provided that gambling is not compulsive, and that losers are not impoverished through participating. Raffles and tombolas are fairly frequent sights at church fund-raising events. Similarly, expecting interest on an investment is permissible – again, so long as the lender is not being exploitative. Many churches are now concerned about ethical investments, and reorganizing their portfolios accordingly. Fair trade is also a present concern in many churches in the West, and congregations can apply to gain formal recognition as a 'fair trade congregation' if they adopt appropriate policies in relation to catering and other purchases.

It is popularly supposed that there is a significant division between Roman Catholics and Protestants on matters of sexual morality. This is not strictly true. All Christian traditions view marriage as the ideal state (outside those religious orders where it is disallowed), being the model that God envisaged for men and women before they were tainted by sin: 'a man will leave his father and mother and be united to his wife, and they will become one flesh' (Genesis 2:24).

The main ground of disagreement, principally between Catholics and Protestants, is about the purpose of marriage, and the extent to which procreation is a requirement. Adam and Eve are told in the Garden of Eden to 'be fruitful and increase in number' (Genesis 1:28), and in Catholic teaching this is taken to mean that the purpose of marriage is to create a family – hence the possibility of procreation must always exist when sexual relationships are entered into. This is the main consideration underlying Roman Catholic teaching on artificial forms of contraception; where a method of contraception is also abortive (for example IUDs and 'morning after' pills), this then constitutes an added objection. Protestants and Anglicans have taken the view that sex can legitimately be for enjoyment as well as for reproduction, and hence it is permissible for couples to engage in sexual activity without having to bring into life children that they may not want.

Traditionally, all branches of mainstream Christianity have taught that sex must be practised exclusively within the confines of marriage, and that adultery and pre-marital sex are wrong. However, as Western attitudes to sex and marriage are changing, some sectors of the Church have come to accept that, for example, couples live together without having made a formal commitment to each other in a marriage ceremony. In 2009 the Church of England gave rise to controversy by offering a 'two in one' ceremony, in which couples could combine their marriage service with the baptism of their children, thus explicitly recognizing and, arguably, condoning the birth of children outside wedlock.

As homosexual partnerships become increasingly accepted in Western society, Christians have had to examine the biblical stance on homosexuality and how to respond to it. Fundamentalists point to prohibitions in the Bible, such as the commandment, 'Do not lie with a man as one lies with a woman; that is detestable' (Leviticus 18:22). Paul appears to endorse this aspect of Jewish law when he writes about God's wrath being shown because, among other wicked deeds, 'Men committed indecent acts with other men' (Romans 1:27). More liberal Christians have suggested that homosexual relationships are alluded to in the Bible (for example David and Jonathan, Ruth and Naomi) without disapproval, or that the Bible is a document that reflects the attitudes of the times and places of its writing, and that subsequent generations of Christians receive 'greater light' as their understanding of their faith progresses. Some have argued that Christian attitudes should not be shaped by individual verses in the Bible, but by the book as a whole. Jesus, for example, is not portrayed as a family man, and even suggests that family life should be sacrificed for the sake of the kingdom (Matthew 19:29). Other issues relating to same-sex partnerships have included the question whether it is acceptable for clergy to be openly gay or lesbian, and whether gay couples might undergo marriage or marriage blessings in church, in ceremonies similar to traditional weddings and wedding blessings. In some countries and states, homosexual partnerships now have legal status, and thus churches that disapprove of such relationships are effectively forcing such couples to turn to the state, rather than the Church, to seal their commitment to each other.

Respect for Life

Although the issue of contraception continues to divide Christians, there is more unanimity on abortion and euthanasia, where divisions tend largely to lie between Christians and secularists. In all traditions, it is held that God, as Creator, has the prerogative to create life, and that men and women should not terminate life, either before birth or in cases where a person is terminally ill and has little quality of life left. Catholics and Orthodox, along with many (but not all) Protestants, hold that life begins at the moment of conception, not the moment of birth or at some arbitrary point in foetal development. God says to Jeremiah, 'Before I formed you in the womb I knew you' (Jeremiah 1:5), and Augustine and subsequent Christian theologians have maintained that conception is the moment at which original sin enters the person. Just as the beginning of life is God's prerogative, God is the one who must decide when it ends, although 'over-zealous' treatment of the terminally ill is not required. A minority of Christians, mainly within the Anglican tradition but also including the Roman Catholic theologian Hans Küng, have argued for change with regard to euthanasia, and many rank-and-file Christian women have sought and obtained abortions.

Human life is not to be spared at any cost, however. Throughout history, Christians have recognized the need to engage in armed combat, with resultant loss of life. The Roman Catholic Church has formulated a number of criteria for a war to be regarded as just. It must be authorized by an appropriate civil authority; it must be waged in defence against 'lasting, grave and certain' damage by an aggressor; it must be a last resort; there must be a likelihood of success; and the evil consequences of war should not outweigh the advantages gained (*Catechism*, 2309). This last criterion has aroused particular concern, the development of nuclear weapons causing many Christians to ask whether the use of modern weaponry could ever justify the results of 'victory'.

Absolutes or Signposts?

In this short chapter it is not possible to give anything more than an outline of how the various strands of Christianity regard the Christian's ethical norms. Changes in societal attitudes, coupled with advances in technology, have caused several areas of the Church's moral teaching to be challenged. Particularly in the Protestant tradition, it has been questioned whether the Church should continue to prescribe moral 'absolutes'. In 1963, Joseph Fletcher (1905–91), an Anglican clergyman, wrote *Situation Ethics: The New Morality*, in which he contended that there are no absolute standards to which one can legitimately be bound in every situation. Even an act such as adultery, he argues, might be permissible: he cites the case of a woman who deliberately became pregnant in order to secure release from a prisoner-of-war camp and be reunited with her family. Fletcher contends that the only absolute is 'love', as Jesus taught: everything else is relative to that, and hence what is right can vary with the situation.

It is significant that situation ethics emerges from within Protestantism, where it is not the practice to codify ethical teachings and present them as having authority over its members. The theory puts the onus of moral decision-making on the individual, informed by the teaching of Jesus and one's conscience. The division between situationism and absolutism may not be as great as it appears: subscribers to both theories would not claim that 'anything goes' in the name of morality. Canon law, in both Roman Catholicism and Orthodoxy, allows for different circumstances necessitating different actions. Situationists would not disagree that moral rules play an important role in moral decision-making. The main ground of the controversy between situationists and absolutists lies in whether the prime justification for moral behaviour lies in divine command, or whether it rests in the consequences right action brings to human beings who are the recipients of love. This contrast continues to mark an important difference between those Christians who want to adhere to conservative traditional values, and those who advocate moral change.

Chapter 7

Women in Christianity

Most religions are patriarchal, and Christianity is no exception. Although Christians know that God is not an old man with a beard, that is how he is depicted in much Christian art, underlining his masculine authority, and he is almost invariably referred to in the male gender. It is God's Son who incarnated, not a daughter, and thus Christianity believes in a male redeemer, and he is referred to as Lord and Master. It is sometimes suggested that the Holy Spirit is the feminine aspect of divinity, but this is inaccurate. The Hebrew word *ruah* is a feminine noun, but the Greek word *pneuma*, which is the New Testament rendering, is neuter, and the Latin *Spiritus* is masculine. Christians may realize, however, that God is beyond gender: as the Church of England's *39 Articles of Religion* states, God is a being 'without body, parts, or passions' (Article I).

All of Jesus' 12 principal disciples were men. The authors of scripture were all male, and most English translations have failed to use inclusive language, using expressions like 'If anyone would come after me, he must deny himself' (Luke 9:23), even though the original Greek is already gender-inclusive. (The King James Version is even more gender-biased with its, 'If any man will come after me...') The Church's scholars, too, have predominately been men, and until Protestants began to make changes, mainly in the twentieth century, the clergy were invariably male. Men have thus defined women's beliefs and roles. In Roman Catholicism and Orthodoxy, women continue to be barred from entering the priesthood, and some Protestant denominations still adopt a traditionalist stance. A casual visit to a church will often confirm the sex-role stereotyping that continues to prevail, with women working in the kitchen, and men fulfilling didactic and hegemonic roles, or performing the more macho tasks like setting up equipment or carrying heavy loads. Even church choirs have sometimes been closed to women, and some continue to be so, since some directors of music prefer to use young boys to sing treble parts, contending that there is a noticeable difference between boys' voices and female ones. Despite this apparent discrimination against women, in the majority of congregations women paradoxically outnumber men significantly.

Christians are agreed that the creation of male and female was within God's purpose. However, the creation narrative appears to suggest that Eve was an indirect creation by God: she is made out of one of Adam's ribs, and with the purpose of being Adam's helper (Genesis 2:18–23). By contrast, Adam is the direct creation, and is already given authority over the Garden of Eden before Eve is brought into existence. Eve was the first to sin, as the first letter to Timothy points out (1 Timothy 2:14). The serpent tempted Eve to eat the forbidden fruit, which she then offered to Adam; thus it was through Eve's sin that Adam fell from grace. The woman, therefore, is the temptress, and the Fall is associated with sexual awareness and lust. Augustine believed that, when God commanded Adam and Eve to 'be fruitful and increase in number' (Genesis 1:28), he intended them simply to reproduce the species, not to enjoy sexual activity, and that in the coming heavenly kingdom, while both sexes will continue to exist, they will no longer feel sexual lust.

The difference between male and female bodies has inevitably been a source of unequal treatment between men and women within Christianity. Much of Catholic scholastic thought derived from Aristotle, who held that women were less capable of reason than men. Saint Thomas Aquinas, following Aristotle's cue, described women as 'deformed men'. The fact that women's bodies function differently in obvious respects led to women being seen as polluting. According to Old Testament law, a menstruating woman was unclean for seven days, defiling anything on which she sat, and polluting anyone with whom she came into contact (Leviticus 15:19–24). The taboo on menstruation was certainly relevant to the resistance to women's ordination in the Church of England. Some opponents thought that a menstruating priest would defile the sanctuary and, worse still, the sacrament, pointing out that one can never know with certainty when a woman might be menstruating.

The male-authored Bible has enabled men to define the role of women within the Christian tradition. In addition to his observations about Adam and Eve, Paul is renowned for his apparently misogynist teachings. Women, he says, should dress modestly at worship, with their heads covered, and should remain silent during worship, only talking to ask their husbands for elucidation if there is something they have failed to understand (1 Corinthians 14:33–5).

The subordination of women extended to home life, not merely to congregational practice. Paul explains that the husband is 'head' of the wife, with Christ as the head of the man. Women should therefore assume a subservient role, obeying their husbands. Such ideas are not discarded first-century practice by any means. Although it is becoming increasingly uncommon, some fundamentalist congregations still insist on women wearing hats in church, and the Church of England's *Book of Common Prayer* contains the bridal promise 'to love, cherish, and to obey, till death us do part' (*BCP*, p. 203). (This version of the marriage service is now rarely used, however, although it still remains an option.)

Although women cannot become priests in the Roman Catholic tradition, monastic orders remain open to them, and many women have sought to become nuns as a way of devoting their lives to God. The monastic life presents celibacy as an ideal for several reasons. First, it can be seen as the antithesis of Adam and Eve accepting sexuality and sexual enjoyment as the norm; a kind of reversal of the Fall and Eve's succumbing to temptation. Parts of the Bible also seem to commend celibacy as a desirable, although not compulsory, state. When Jesus speaks about the responsibilities of marriage and the severe constraints surrounding legitimate divorce, his disciples comment, 'If this is the situation between a husband and wife, it is better not to marry' (Matthew 19:10). Jesus replies that some men have gone so far as to become eunuchs for the sake of the kingdom, and that 'others have renounced marriage because of the kingdom of heaven. The one who can accept this should accept it' (Matthew 19:11–12). Paul appears to have been unmarried (1 Corinthians 7:8), and commends the unmarried state as being desirable, allowing those who are free of marital responsibilities and sexual desires to dedicate themselves to prayer. He views marriage as a second-best alternative, being preferable to 'burning with passion' (1 Corinthians 7:36).

Although the monastic life appears to involve living in a closed community, this is not necessarily so. Monasteries and nunneries have served the community by providing clinics and schools. Hildegard of Bingen (1098–1179) founded monasteries at Rupertsberg and Eibingen in Germany, where she composed works on botany and medicine, as well as songs, plays and poems. Although the Church did not permit her to preach, since she was a woman, she was able to recount her visionary experiences, which continue to inspire the faithful. In more recent times, Mother Teresa of Calcutta (1910–97) was particularly renowned for her Missionaries of Charity, which she founded in Calcutta in 1950, offering help to the orphaned, the sick and the dying. Hildegard and Mother Teresa were both beatified – a preliminary step towards full canonization. Such honour by the Church demonstrates that women are by no means barred from attaining sainthood, and indeed the Roman Catholic Church acknowledges many female saints. However, some Christians will point out that canonization is decided by an exclusively male hierarchy, leaving women without a voice on such matters.

Feminine Divine Imagery

Feminine images of holiness are most markedly seen in the devotion paid to the Virgin Mary in the Roman Catholic and Eastern Orthodox traditions. Protestants are opposed to veneration of Mary, however, accepting the Reformation teaching that the believer has direct access to God. They would resist any practice that suggests that Christ may not have achieved his atoning work unaided, fearing that veneration of Mary might detract from devotion to Christ. Nonetheless, all traditions hold that Jesus Christ was 'born of the Virgin Mary' and connect the belief to Isaiah's prophecy, that 'The virgin will be with child and will give birth to a son, and will call him Immanuel' (Isaiah 7:14). Gabriel's announcement to Mary that she is 'highly favoured' and that she will bear the Christ-child places her in a role that reverses the position of Eve. As Saint Irenaeus wrote, 'The knot of Eve's disobedience was untied by Mary's obedience: what the virgin Eve bound through her disbelief, Mary loosened by her faith' (*Catechism*, 494). Unlike Eve, Mary is the perfect obedient woman, 'full of grace', the perfect mother, who is the embodiment of chastity and purity, enabling Jesus to come into the world as the 'Second Adam', born without original sin and leading a life of perfect obedience to his Father.

Mary also represents the Church. She was present when the Holy Spirit descended at Pentecost, the date of the Church's inception (Acts 1:14), and, being Christ's mother, is the mother of the redeemed. Roman Catholicism and Orthodoxy typically portray her artistically in her maternal role, and paintings and icons of the Madonna and Child are well known. (*Madonna* means 'my lady' in Italian.) Because

Jesus Christ is held to have been fully God as well as fully human, Mary has been given the title *theotokos*, or Mother of God, and this is used as a form of address within Catholicism and Orthodoxy. Orthodoxy also refers to her as *panagia* – 'all holy'. The title *theotokos* was officially conferred on her at the Council of Ephesus (431 CE), which was the occasion for much popular rejoicing. Ephesus attracted a reputation for its goddess worship before the arrival of Christianity, and Mary thus fulfilled the role of the goddess. The title 'Mother of God' is disliked in Protestant circles, however, although it is nonetheless part of the tradition that led to the formation of the Christian creeds.

The veneration of Mary can be traced back to early Church Fathers, and arguably to the Bible itself. Luke records that a woman called out to Jesus amidst a crowd, 'Blessed is the mother who gave you birth and nursed you' (Luke 11:27). In Orthodoxy and Catholicism, Mary is accorded the role of intercessor, and devotees in both these traditions petition the Virgin Mary, asking her to pray for them. The Western tradition went further, and attributed to her an 'immaculate conception'. It is important to note that the Immaculate Conception is not the same as the Virgin Birth, although the two doctrines are frequently confused, both inside and outside the Church. The doctrine of the Immaculate Conception means that from the very moment of Mary's conception by her mother Anne she was free from original sin. (Mary's parents, Anne and Joachim, are not mentioned in the Bible, but appear in apocryphal writings.) This doctrine was deemed a prerequisite for ensuring that Jesus was born as a perfect human, so that he could be the perfect sacrifice, the 'lamb without blemish or defect' (1 Peter 1:19). In 1854, Pope Pius IX declared this an official Roman Catholic doctrine, it having been held for many centuries previously.

Allied to the doctrine of the Virgin Birth is the 'perpetual virginity' of Mary. The Catholic Church holds that, not only was Mary a virgin when she conceived Jesus, but she remained a virgin throughout the rest of her life. Such a claim may seem problematic, since Matthew and Luke record that Jesus had brothers and sisters (Matthew 13:56; Luke 8:20). The *Catechism of the Catholic Church* explains, however, that these were the children of another woman called Mary: there are several women of that name in the New Testament. The Roman Church further declared that on her death Mary's body did not remain on earth, but was taken up ('assumed') directly into heaven. This teaching is known as the Dogma of the Assumption. It was formalized as late as 1950, but it was already accepted by the faithful for many centuries previously. Mary is also given the title 'Mediatrix', indicating that she has a mediatorial role, acting as intercessor on behalf of the faithful, as well as having an important role in the world's salvation. Irenaeus wrote, 'Being obedient she became the cause of salvation for herself and for the whole human race' (quoted in *Catechism*, 494). More controversial is the application of the title 'Co-Redemptrix' to Mary. The Roman Catholic Church acknowledges the vital role that Mary played in the world's redemption. Mary responded to Gabriel's call, was present beneath the cross at Jesus' crucifixion, and was a witness of the empty tomb. However, the Church stops back from assigning her an equal role, acknowledging that Christ holds a unique mediatorial role between God and the world and that it was Christ's suffering and death, not Mary's obedience, that atoned for sin. The controversy about Mary as Co-Redemptrix continues, however: in 2008 five cardinals petitioned Pope Benedict XVI to approve the titles 'Co-Redemptrix' and 'Mediatrix', following a petition, started in 1993, which attracted over six million signatures.

Opinion among feminists is divided on whether the image of Mary is helpful to the cause of women. On the one hand, Mary provides a feminine focus for devotion amidst a religion that is male-dominated and that does not include goddess worship. The emphasis on Mary in the Christian story also acknowledges the role of women in the history of the world's redemption, and helps to provide status for women. Also, as the anti-typical Eve, Mary embodies the virtues, providing a role model for women, which differs from the sinner and temptress. On the other hand, the role model that Mary provides is precisely the difficulty for some feminist writers. Mary's role is maternal, suggesting that the ideal woman is the child-bearer and the mother. She is also paradoxically celibate, suggesting monastic celibacy as the ideal state. She is submissive, acquiescing instantly to Gabriel's announcement, thus underlining the submissiveness of the female to the male. As goddess, Mary has only a subordinate role: she is not divine; she is not the Redemptrix, or even the Co-Redemptrix of the world. Nonetheless, with the exception of the Protestant tradition, many women – not to mention men – find Mary an appropriate object of devotion and help in their spiritual life.

Feminist Interpretations of Christianity

Reaction against Christianity's patriarchal nature has generated a branch of theology known as feminist theology. Some of the writers in the field, such as Mary Daly and Daphne Hampson, have taken the view that Christianity is irretrievably sexist, and should be abandoned. Others, such as Mary C. Grey, Elisabeth Schüssler Fiorenza, Sally McFague, Rosemary Radford Ruether and Phyllis Trible, believe that it is capable of being reformed and interpreted in such a way as to empower women, rather than to legitimate their often submissive role. The problems that these writers find with Christianity's treatment of women are various. God is portrayed as male, and masculine metaphors are used to describe him, such as 'King', 'Lord' and 'Father', and he is endowed with 'masculine' qualities such as power and might. He is the warrior God who leads his people into battle and gives them victory. The role of women in the Bible and in the Church's history, they argue, has been downplayed. Women are rendered 'invisible', either by being omitted from the narrative altogether, or by being unnamed. (Jesus talks to 'a Samaritan woman' and heals 'a woman' with a haemorrhage, yet Zacchaeus the tax-collector and Simon the Pharisee are named.) The language used in the Bible and in much of the Church's liturgy tends to be exclusive, employing the masculine gender. The *Book of Common Prayer* opens with the biblical quotation, 'When the wicked man turneth away from his wickedness ...' (*BCP* Order for Morning Prayer; Ezekiel 18:27) – one of many examples – and hymns and anthems similarly use 'man' when 'people' is meant. The *Catechism of the Catholic Church* also fails to use inclusive language, despite the fact that it was revised in 1994.

The agenda of feminist theologians is to free the Christian faith from its traditionally andocentric character, and to develop new ways of questioning and interpreting the Bible and tradition. Fiorenza suggests four hermeneutic principles that can profitably be applied to the biblical narrative. First, there is a 'hermeneutic of suspicion', which means that one may assume at the outset that the text has been written from an andocentric standpoint or from andocentric motives. Second, there is 'proclamation': any interpretation must be one that can be used for today. The third principle is 'remembrance', in the sense of bearing in mind the situation in which women of today find themselves. Finally, 'creative actualization' is an imaginative and constructive activity in which a more comprehensive view of women can be worked out from fragmentary evidence.

The activity of these feminist writers is sometimes described as the 'recovery of a lost tradition', and it is often pointed out that the role of women in the early Jesus movement is greater than has traditionally been assumed. Although women were not among the 12 apostles, Jesus nonetheless appears to have had female disciples. Mary, the sister of Martha and Lazarus, sat at Jesus' feet listening to his teaching (Luke 10:39), and Mary Magdalene called the risen Jesus 'Rabbouni', meaning 'Teacher' (John 20:16). Women were among the last to leave Jesus' cross, and were first at the empty tomb. They were the first witnesses of the resurrection, and their names are set on record by way of evidence: 'Mary Magdalene, Mary the mother of James and Joses, and the mother of Zebedee's sons' (Matthew 27:56). Given the importance of the resurrection and the prevailing societal view of women, the Gospel writers might have been expected to insert the names of men in their place, to secure greater credibility, but they did not do so. Women were among the early leaders of the Church, and are frequently named in Paul's letters, and women prophets were recognized (Acts 21: 9). The first martyrs included women: Felicity and Perpetua at Carthage around 203 CE.

Sometimes women need to be 'reclaimed' from patriarchy. Lisa Isherwood argues, for example, that Mary Magdalene has been andocentrically misrepresented. Traditionally, she is regarded as a harlot, assumed to be guilty of sexual impropriety, and delivered by Jesus from possession by seven demons. While this last point of detail is authentic (Mark 16:9), Mary Magdalene is nowhere portrayed in the Bible as a prostitute, and she was the first person to receive a commission from the risen Christ to 'go and tell' (John 20:17).

Christian feminists can be divided into two categories: reformists and reconstructionists. The former simply want to see better Bible translations, more use of inclusive language in the Church's liturgy and hymnody, and more women in leadership roles. The latter wish to go further and discover a new theological underpinning. Many of them view feminist theology as a form of liberation theology, releasing an oppressed sector of society from those who dominate them. Most emphasize that their theology should emanate from experience, from the questions and issues that confront women today, rather than from abstract metaphysical doctrines. These experiences will differ from one environment to another, and hence one can expect feminist theology to assume a variety of forms of expression.

Feminist theologians do not normally want to substitute the term 'goddess' for 'God', or to refer to God as 'Mother' instead of 'Father', but seek rather to counterbalance the unduly masculine imagery that pertains to God. Occasionally, one discovers female imagery being applied to God, for example in Isaiah, when God says, 'But now, like a woman in childbirth, I cry out ...' (Isaiah 42:14). The Book of Job compares divine creativity to a womb giving birth: 'From whose womb comes the ice? Who gives birth to the frost from the heavens?' (Job 38:29). Jesus compares himself with a mother hen: 'how often I have longed to gather your children together, as a hen gathers her chicks under her wings' (Matthew 23:37). Rather than substitute female for male imagery, some feminists have suggested other appellations for God. Sally McFague proposes 'lover' and 'friend' as metaphors that are gender-neutral and do not suggest masculine domination over the feminine. However, as Ruether acknowledges, 'we have no adequate name for the true God/ess, the "I am who I shall become"' (Ruether, 1983: 71; quoted in Isherwood and McEwan, p. 149). This is an allusion to Moses' asking God's name and being given the enigmatic answer 'I AM' (Exodus 3:14).

More problematic is the concept of the 'kingdom of God', which is firmly embedded in Jesus' teaching, and which connotes patriarchal authority. Relatively few parables of the kingdom involve women, and the first two of these examples suggest a traditional female-stereotypical role. The kingdom is compared to yeast, which a woman puts in dough (Matthew 13:33), ten bridesmaids await a bridegroom (Matthew 25:1–13); a woman hunts for a lost coin until she finds it (Luke 15:8–10); and a widow persists in seeking justice from an unjust judge (Luke 18:1–8). There is no agreed answer to this problem: the elimination of the phrase would certainly involve massive reappraisal of scripture, not to mention prayer and hymnody. More amenable to feminist theology is the notion of the Trinity, however. Although the masculine gender is used to characterize two of the three members, their relationship is less suggestive of male domination, but incorporates a social relationship, a kind of network, which some feminists welcome.

Women's Ordination

Particularly within the Protestant tradition, where monasticism and female divine imagery are missing, some women have felt that women should be entitled to equal status with men, including the right to become fully ordained as members of the clergy, to preach, and to preside over the sacraments. In 1667 Margaret Fell (1614–1702) published a pamphlet entitled *Women's speaking justified, proved and allowed of by the Scriptures*. Margaret Fell married George Fox, and with several others founded the Religious Society of Friends, also known as the Quakers. As part of the radical Protestant Reformation, the Quakers were – and still are – a lay organization. In their endeavour to establish a form of religion that came from the heart, they removed the external trappings of religion to the extent of doing away with clergy and sacraments. Margaret Fell's campaigning was not therefore for the ordination of women, but for the right of women to preach. Some sixty supporters of Fox – they became known as the Valiant Sixty – travelled throughout England, as well as to other parts of Europe and North America, preaching their faith. Some of the sixty were women, and many of the group suffered imprisonment and corporal punishment for acting contrary to the established religion. In a Quaker meeting, the congregation remains in silence, which may be interrupted when a member feels prompted by the Holy Spirit to speak. Speaking at the meeting is known as 'giving ministry', and men and women alike are allowed to contribute.

The question of who was the first woman to be ordained is complex and slightly controversial. The term 'ordination' has somewhat different meanings in different denominations, and one can be ordained to different offices. Some denominations are entirely lay-led, such as the Brethren, but a lay leadership does not necessarily mean that women are eligible for leadership roles. In Protestant churches one can be ordained as a deacon, an elder, a preacher or a minister who can preside over the sacraments – there is considerable variation according to tradition. (The word 'deacon' also carries different meanings in different denominations.) When the Freewill Baptist Church (an American denomination originating in Carolina in the late eighteenth century) ordained Nancy Gove Cram (1776–1816) in 1810, her ministry was to preach to the Oneida Indians. She could not celebrate Holy Communion, or even baptize her converts. Being authorized to preach, however, was an unprecedented achievement for her, and for a number of other women evangelists whom the denomination authorized.

In some cases, a woman's ordination might be recognized by a congregation or a part of a denomination, but rejected more widely. This was the case with Antoinette Brown (1825–1921), who was ordained by the Congregational Church of South Butler, New York, in 1853. Since this was a Congregationalist Church, the ordination was approved by the congregation, but it did not entitle her to officiate elsewhere. Brown eventually moved away from Congregationalism, becoming a Unitarian. Meanwhile, the Universalist Church had ordained Olympia Brown (1835–1926), who is frequently cited as the first woman to become ordained (although Universalism is not regarded as a mainstream Christian denomination). Olympia Brown's ordination in 1863, unlike Antoinette Brown's, was accepted denomination-wide. The Salvation Army, founded by William Booth in 1865, from its inception admitted men and women equally to all ranks. However, there is no ordination as such in the Salvation Army, and there are no sacraments, but women, like men, are permitted to preach. There is a regulation, however, that forbids a man from marrying a woman of higher rank.

The first woman's full ordination in a mainstream denomination was Anna Howard Shaw in 1880, by the Methodist Protestant Church (now merged with other US Methodist bodies as the United Methodist Church). In 1888, Louisa Woosley (1862–1952) was ordained by the Nolin Presbytery of the Cumberland Presbyterian Church. Her ordination was challenged by other presbyteries of the denomination, but she succeeded in retaining her role as an ordained minister, owing to her own presbytery's loyalty. She wrote a book *Shall Women Preach?* in 1891.

The first half of the twentieth century witnessed some further progress with women's ordination. When the (Pentecostalist) Assemblies of God were founded in 1914, women pastors were appointed, and in 1917 the Congregationalist Church in England and Wales appointed its first women ministers. From 1920 some Baptist denominations followed suit. Later in the century, Florence Li Tim Oi was ordained as an Anglican priest in Hong Kong. This was an emergency measure, but it set a precedent for what was to come. It was only in the second half of the twentieth century, however, that the ordination of women became commonplace. The United States tended to lead the rest of the world, with Methodists, Presbyterians and some Lutheran Churches in Scandinavia paving the way. From the mid-1970s the ordination of Episcopalian women priests had begun in the US.

It was not until 1992 that the Church of England's General Synod formally approved the ordination of women, and the first ordinations took place two years later. Not everyone was in agreement, however, and parishes were allowed to make 'alternative episcopal arrangements' where the decision was deemed unacceptable. This arrangement involved the parish being removed from the supervision of the bishop who had authority over the geographically defined diocese, and coming under the care of a 'provincial episcopal visitor' – popularly known as a 'flying bishop'. Three 'flying bishops' were appointed to oversee dissenting congregations in various parts of England. The episcopal visitors would oversee their parishes, visiting them when necessary, and would be responsible for appointments of clergy in their geographically fragmented provinces. Above all, they would not ordain women or permit women clergy who had been ordained elsewhere to have oversight over their congregations.

The opponents of women's ordination adduced several arguments in their defence. The priest, it was argued, is the representative of Christ. Therefore, how can a woman represent Christ, who was a man? Jesus' 12 apostles were all male, and Paul's clear instructions to the Corinthians and to Timothy forbid women speaking or assuming positions of authority. Additionally, there was a (probably genuine) concern about denominational stability. Since women's ordination is controversial, any decision in favour of women's ordination was likely to cause schism. It was feared that some denominations might actually split (although, to the author's knowledge, this has not occurred), or at least have significant numbers of congregations that were 'no go' areas for prospective women clergy. A wider issue was ecumenism. Since Roman Catholicism and Eastern Orthodoxy remain opposed to women clergy, the ordination of women was likely to prove damaging to ecumenical relationships. Intercommunion would not be possible if the celebrant was a woman, and even the permission for women to preside over Holy Communion indicated a significantly different view of the sacraments on the part of Anglicans and Protestants.

In response to these traditionalist arguments, supporters of women's ordination pointed out that maleness was only one characteristic of Christ. He was also Jewish, Aramaic-speaking, Galilean, and bearded: did Christ's representatives need to possess all these characteristics also? If not, why single out gender as the one attribute that had to match Christ's nature? Christ represented humanity by redeeming the entire world – both men and women – by his atoning sacrifice on the cross. If a male redeemer can represent both genders, why cannot both genders represent Christ by presiding over the sacrament? Regarding the apostles, the 'twelve' may indeed have been male, but Jesus also had female disciples. One commentator notes that, of the ten disciples who are described in some detail (some of the twelve have only their names recorded), five are women (Robinson, 2005). Concerning Paul's statements, supporters of women's ordination have pointed out that the letters to Timothy are inauthentic. There is also dispute about what precisely Paul meant when he apparently forbade women to speak in Church. Some have argued that he is quoting another view, with which he disagrees, pointing out that the prohibition is not consistent with what Paul says elsewhere; others suggest that the prohibition is on prophesying rather than teaching; a further suggestion is that he is only referring to married women, since he advises them to address questions to their husbands; it has even been suggested that Paul is forbidding idle chatter during public worship. Again, it has been argued that Paul reflects the first-century attitudes of his time, from which the Church has now moved on.

Regarding denominational stability and ecumenical relationships, there can be no doubt that women's ordination has been unsettling. In 2000, following the ordination of two women deacons in the Church of Pakistan, the United Presbyterian Church of Pakistan (a breakaway organization) attempted to persuade a civil court in Lahore that the bishop's act of ordaining them was in contempt. Following the admission of women to the priesthood in the Church of England, it was not uncommon for some members to refuse to receive the sacrament from a woman, or to transfer their allegiance to a congregation that was less sympathetic to women's ordination. Following the 1992 decision, some argued that a decision by the General Synod to ordain women was insufficient: such a decision had to be taken by the whole Church, and not merely a part of it. Some dissenting clergy felt that their consciences could not allow them to remain in the Church of England, and a number were able to cross over to the Roman Catholic Church.

Opposition to women's ordination in the Church of England became organized. In 1992, Forward in Faith (FiF) was set up with the aim of upholding traditional teachings and practices in the denomination. This included, but was not confined to, women's ordination. The organization's Code of Practice, adopted in 1994, may seem moderate:

> We seriously doubt that women so ordained are priests in the Church of God; but we accept that we may prove mistaken. It is doubt about the validity of the orders conferred, and not certainty as to their invalidity, which requires us to distance ourselves from them. (Forward in Faith, 1994)

Forward in Faith's point is that it is not sufficient for such ordinations to be valid: there must be certainty that this is so, otherwise congregations cannot be assured of the validity of the sacraments. The situation is further exacerbated by the possibility of the appointment of women bishops. If a woman bishop's ordination is not valid, then neither is the ordination of those she ordains, and, since it is difficult to ascertain the lineage of a priest's ordination, women bishops would introduce a 'taint' into the Church, and one could seldom be sure of the validity of any priest's ordination or the sacraments any male priest dispenses. Forward in Faith therefore recommends the laity to join congregations with alternative episcopal oversight, where possible; if this cannot be done, they should avoid churches with female priests, and should ensure that they donate only to churches with alternative episcopal care (or else directly to FiF).

The campaign for women's ordination is therefore by no means over. The appointment of women bishops is the next goal. There are now women bishops in the Episcopal Church of the United States, and also in New Zealand. In 2008 the General Synod of the Church of England voted on the issue but, although the House of Bishops and the House of Clergy had the required two-thirds majority, the House of Laity did not reach this target, although most lay representatives were in favour.

There are women, as well as men, who would like to see the ordination of women in the Roman Catholic Church. At the time of writing, the prospects are not encouraging. In 1988 the papal encyclical *Mulieris Dignitatem* ('On the Dignity and Vocation of Women') set out to respond to the challenge of feminism. It affirmed that, just as Jesus' attitudes to women did not conform to the norms of his time, so the Church should not accommodate itself to secular feminist ideology. Instead, women should discover the true meaning of femininity, rather than endeavour to assume male characteristics. Women, Pope John Paul II affirmed, were not of lesser dignity, as is evidenced by the Virgin Mary, who represents simultaneously the two ways in which women can gain fulfilment: motherhood, and virginity for the sake of the kingdom (the monastic life). In 1994 the papal document *Ordinatio Sacerdotalis* addressed specifically the issue of women's ordination. Commenting on recent attempts to open up the subject to debate, the Pope silenced further discussion by stating: 'I declare that the Church has no authority whatsoever to confer priestly ordination on women and that this judgment is to be definitively held by all the Church's faithful' (*Ordinatio Sacerdotalis*, 1994).

The faithful are reminded that to deny ordination to women is not to downgrade their value: the Virgin Mary was not made a priest, but nonetheless fulfilled an essential role in the world's salvation, being the Mother of God and the Mother of the Church. Women in the Roman Catholic Church can now be altar servers, may lead prayers, and may officiate at a service of worship (but not the Mass) if a priest is unavailable.

Orthodoxy is equally opposed to women priests, for very similar reasons to those of Roman Catholicism: the example of Jesus and church tradition. Those seeking priesthood must do so on God's terms, not their own, which entails not being swayed by secular ideologies. Orthodoxy acknowledges that there can be women saints, even equal to apostles – for example, Mary Magdalene. At various points throughout the ages women have been admitted to the diaconate, which is generally accepted as an ordained office, since admission involves the laying on of hands. Women deacons have assisted in baptism and chrismation, and also the anointing of sick, in order to avoid a male priest having physical contact with the female body where the candidates are women. The Russian Orthodox Church has probably retained this office since its inception, and in 2004 the Holy Synod of the Orthodox Church of Greece restored the office of the female diaconate.

Why More Women than Men?

Although Christian feminists may see signs of progress with the development of feminist theology, the ordination of women within most of the Protestant tradition, and the increasing involvement of women in the running of congregations and in the liturgy, Christianity still remains patriarchal and male-led. Why is it, then, that at an average Sunday service, significantly more women attend than men? Linda Woodhead (2004) suggests a number of reasons. Christianity, she argues, commends 'womanly' virtues, such as love, gentleness, obedience. It teaches that devotion is more important than gaining worldly power, and thus 'empowers' women. Thus they can remain in a servile role, both at church and in everyday life, and serve God with erotic piety. Where women have engaged in social campaigning, such work has involved issues such as temperance, which seek to curtail male machismo. As far as men are concerned, it is not that their work prevents them from attending church. Their quest for material prosperity, however, may suggest different values from those that the Church teaches.

Chapter 8

Life and Death

The apostle Paul wrote, 'For to me, to live is Christ and to die is gain' (Philippians 1:21). Christianity speaks positively about both life and death. For the vast majority of Christians, the Christian life does not involve austerity or self-torment. The Bible repeatedly exhorts Christians to be joyful, and new converts to Christianity have frequently testified to feelings of joy and increased happiness on accepting Christ. The only pleasures that a Christian is obliged to give up are sinful ones. Having written a letter reprimanding the church at Corinth, which appears to have caused offence to the Christians there, Paul writes in his second letter that he does not regret causing them sorrow, because it led to their repentance. 'Godly sorrow' is good, but 'worldly sorrow brings death' (2 Corinthians 7:10).

Most Christians recognize that their faith does not afford a life of constant pleasure, but even in affliction they can find consolation in Christ. The expression 'in Christ' is a key phrase for understanding the Christian life. To quote Paul again, 'if anyone is in Christ, he is a new creation; the old has gone, the new has come!' (2 Corinthians 5:17). Christianity offers a new life, consisting of 'death to sin' and 'newness of life' in Christ. The believer is in Christ and Christ is in the believer, in a symbiotic relationship. Christ's presence is mediated through the Church, and hence embracing the Christian faith entails belonging to a community of Christian believers.

This, of course, is a description of an ideal practising Christian. Clearly, there are degrees of commitment to Christianity. There are many 'cultural Christians', who might celebrate Christmas by attending a carol service, get married in a church and have their children baptized. Some clergy are judgemental of them, while others recognize, like Augustine, that one cannot readily distinguish the true Christians from the false by looking at the earthly characteristics. A committed Christian would attend church on a weekly basis. Half a century ago it was a mark of piety to attend twice a Sunday, but – at least in twenty-first century Britain – only a small percentage of people do so now, and many churches have given up holding evening services. In Roman Catholicism, failure to attend Mass at Easter without good reason would be regarded as a wilful rejection of the Christian faith, and could result in excommunication. Private and household devotions, involving prayer and Bible study, are encouraged, although – with the possible exception of evangelical Protestant churches – this practice seems largely to have died out. Ignorance of scripture has become a source of concern to religious leaders.

We have already examined the Christian lifestyle in terms of its ethical standards (see Chapter 6). However, being 'in Christ' involves more than simply leading a moral life. The life of the Church enables Christians to dedicate their lives, and particularly the key events in them, to Christ. As well as inviting Christ to participate in their lives, Christians also, through the Church, participate in the life of Christ. The Church thus seeks to bring together the life of Christ and the believer's own life. This is done in two principal ways: first, by the Church's liturgical calendar, and second, by the celebration of life-cycle rites ('life events' as the Church of England's website prefers to call them) within the context of the Church.

The liturgical calendar provides an opportunity for Christians not only to remember, but also to participate in, the events in Jesus' life. Even something as seemingly simple as a nativity play can be seen as an attempt by the actors to appropriate the Christmas story for themselves. An Easter vigil is an attempt not merely to recapture the events of the first Good Friday through to Easter morning, but to place oneself within the Easter experience. The Eucharist (or Holy Communion) offers the opportunity for believers to re-enact Jesus' last meal with his disciples, but it also anticipates the future hope of the 'celestial banquet' that is to be expected in heaven: 'You proclaim the Lord's death until he comes' (1 Corinthians 11:26). On this side of death, the believer cannot be part of this celestial banquet, but a small taste of it, as it were, reaches down from heaven in the morsels of bread and wine that are dispensed during the sacrament.

The Christian calendar has a cyclical progression, unlike human existence which is linear, with a beginning and an end. In contrast to Eastern religions, which believe in cycles of births and rebirths, Christianity holds that each human has but one life to live, and that this one life is decisive in determining one's eternal destiny. Christians do not typically believe in the pre-existence of the soul, although pre-existence is taught by the Latter-day Saints and was a doctrine held by the Church Father Origen (c. 185–c. 254). Origen's views tended to be on the edge of acceptability, which explains why he was never canonized.

The main events in human existence are birth, (usually) marriage, and death, and these life events are marked within the context of the Church's liturgy. For the majority of Christians, formally joining the Church is an important event in their lives, and it is marked by confirmation – more usually called 'admission' in Protestant circles. With the exception of the Baptists and Pentecostalists, baptism is administered to babies, acknowledging the child's membership of the Christian community. Some Baptist and Pentecostal churches offer baby blessings – also called dedications or 'namings' – to mark the presence of a new life and to enable the parents to undertake to bring up their newborn child in the faith. ('Naming' is a slight misnomer, of course, since registering a child's name is normally a civil affair.)

Church Membership

In the Orthodox churches, a baby is considered to be a full member of the Church from the moment of baptism. Obviously a young child cannot take on any of the responsibilities of membership, but he or she is eligible to receive Holy Communion, and it is not an uncommon sight to see children being brought up during the Divine Liturgy to partake of the bread and wine. Baptism, which in Orthodoxy is done by immersion, not sprinkling, is therefore accompanied by the second of the life-cycle rites: chrismation, which involves anointing the child's forehead with oil. Oil has symbolic meaning in the Bible, being used for the consecration of kings and priests. The first letter of Peter describes the community of Christians as 'a chosen people, a royal priesthood' (1 Peter 2:9), indicating the special privilege that is accredited to those who belong to the Christian faith. In ancient times, athletes also used oil to lubricate themselves in preparation for competitions. Both Paul and the writer to the Hebrews compare the Christian with a race that has to be run (1 Corinthians 9:24; Hebrews 12:1). The prize, Paul assures the Corinthians, is not the type of crown that was awarded to the winner, but (metaphorically) an everlasting one.

The Christian life is often compared to a journey. The flight of the Israelites from Egypt to the promised land of Canaan, for example, is frequently used in the Church's preaching, theological writing and hymnody as an analogy of the Christian life. The Israelites' journey through the Sinai desert brought its highs and lows. Sometimes God's people were trusting, sometimes they doubted Moses' leadership. At times they bravely endured hardship, at other times they became impatient with their lot. They received God's law at Mount Sinai, but were immediately tempted to follow other gods. They even came to doubt whether the Promised Land was attainable. However, they were always guided by God, who directed them through a pillar of cloud during the day and a pillar of fire at night (Exodus 13:21). The comparisons with living the Christian life in the twenty-first century need no explanation. The famous hymn 'Guide me, O thou great Jehovah' includes the lines:

Let the fire and cloudy pillar
Lead me all my journey through.

Roman Catholicism and Anglicanism separate the rite of baptism from the rite of 'confirmation', as they prefer to call it. When children are considered to be old enough to understand the Christian faith, which obviously they cannot do as infants undergoing baptism, they are admitted to full membership. Candidates for confirmation are often adults, who may have found the Christian faith later in life, or who have simply postponed their decision to seek admission to the Church. Baptism is always a requirement for confirmation, and must be administered before anyone can proceed to it. A period of preparation is required, in the course of which the candidate receives instruction in the faith, and the rite involves publicly expressing one's commitment to the Christian faith, chrismation, followed by the opportunity to receive one's first communion. Since Baptist and Pentecostal churches do not practise infant baptism, baptism by immersion marks one's decision to become a member of the Church. In other forms of Protestantism, candidates are admitted by affirming their faith and taking vows of commitment, normally during public worship.

Marriage

For most Christians, the next rite of passage is marriage, unless one is entering monastic orders in which marriage is disallowed. Monks, nuns and Roman Catholic priests and Orthodox bishops may not marry, but marriage is freely permitted for Protestant ministers. Marriage is regarded as a sacrament in the Roman Catholic and Orthodox traditions, but not among Protestants, who point out that Jesus did not institute marriage or declare it an obligation for his followers. As far as we know, Jesus remained unmarried, and claims that Mary Magdalene was his wife or lover are highly speculative, to say the least. However, Jesus' approval of the institution is shown in the Gospel of John, where it is recorded that he accepted an invitation to a wedding at Cana, and that his first miracle was to turn 150 gallons of water into the finest wine for the wedding banquet (John 2:1–11)! The story is frequently referred to in marriage ceremonies, reminding the couple of Christ's presence in their marriage.

The institution of marriage is held to go back to the beginning of creation, when God is said to have created humankind as male and female, and instructed them to 'Be fruitful and increase in number; fill the earth and subdue it' (Genesis 1:28). The most obvious purpose of marriage is procreation and the setting up of family life, although the Church recognizes the existence of other benefits, such as friendship, mutual support and pursuit of common interests. Most Christian couples marry within a church, and many who lack strong church connections want 'a church wedding', perhaps to satisfy a spark of spirituality, or perhaps because they like the beauty and atmosphere of a church ceremony. It is not necessary to be baptized to gain permission to marry in church, although the Church of England expects couples to have attended the church regularly for six months, unless they already live in the parish. Church weddings in Britain normally combine the religious and the civil requirements involved in conferring legal validity on the marriage. In some other countries separate civil registration is required, and the couple would fulfil this obligation either before or after the church ceremony, as required. In the Roman Catholic Church a Eucharist can, optionally, be incorporated into the wedding ceremony: this is known as a Nuptial Mass.

In a church marriage ceremony the wedding couple are reminded of Jesus' teachings on marriage. On one occasion when the Pharisees asked Jesus about divorce, he reminded them of the creation story, in which God tells Adam and Eve that 'the two will become one flesh' (Mark 10:8). The Church of England's wedding vows include the words, 'All that I have I share with you', which both the bride and bridegroom affirm, indicating a complete sharing of possessions. The marriage vows include the acceptance of one's spouse, 'forsaking all others' – a promise of fidelity. Although the Old Testament records that the patriarchs and some of the kings had several marriage partners and concubines, such a lifestyle belongs to the Old Covenant, not the New. The vows also include the words, 'till death us do part'. This clause highlights two points about marriage. First, it is lifelong; despite 'sequential monogamy' sometimes being championed as the Western societal norm, the Christian marriage vow is not 'as long as our love shall last'. Second, marriage ends at death. In contrast with the Latter-day Saints, mainstream Christianity does not teach that marriage is eternal. Mark's Gospel recounts an incident in which the Sadducees pose a conundrum about a woman who was widowed seven times, enquiring which husband would be her partner in heaven. Jesus' response is, 'When the dead rise, they will neither marry nor be given in marriage; they will be like the angels in heaven' (Mark 12:25).

The Christian ideal is for sex to be reserved for life within marriage: extra-marital sex is a violation of the prohibition on adultery. At the marriage service, the proclamation that the couple are husband and wife is typically followed by Jesus' words, 'Those whom God has joined together let no one put asunder' (Matthew 19:6). Pre-marital as well as extra-marital sex is officially discouraged, although it has become increasingly accepted that this is an ideal rather than the norm. A recent survey indicated that 90 per cent of married Americans had pre-marital sex; the incidence among evangelical Protestants was slightly lower, at 80 per cent (Regnerus, 2009). Despite the recognition that marriage is for life, divorce is not uncommon among Christians. Perhaps surprisingly, divorce rates are highest in the USA's Bible Belt, the reasons for which are not wholly comprehensible. According to recent surveys, 34 per cent of 'non-denominational' evangelical Protestants (that is, those who are not affiliated to a denomination) have previously been divorced; 29 per cent of Baptists, and 25 per cent of mainline Protestants. This compares with 21 per cent of Catholics, Lutherans and atheists (the same rate for each) (Barna, 2008). Most Protestant denominations permit the remarriage of divorcees, despite their previous wedding vows, but not Roman Catholicism (where divorce is not officially recognized, let alone permitted). In the Anglican tradition, remarriage is at the clergy's discretion. Clearly, these high divorce rates are matters of concern, and most denominations now organize pre-marital counselling sessions, in the hopes that couples will be encouraged to recognize the commitments involved in marriage. The Roman Catholic Church insists on attendance at such sessions before proceeding with a wedding.

Death

The final life event is inevitably death. Even those who have little or no connection with a church will usually want the services of religion when a friend or relative dies. Although some humanists have endeavoured to provide alternative secular rites, a Christian funeral is usually sought, unless the family practises some other faith. Where a death is anticipated, a member of the clergy can be present to offer comfort to the dying person. The use of consecrated oil to anoint the sick and the dying is a common practice within the Orthodox, Roman Catholic and some parts of the Anglican tradition. This is not favoured by Protestants, however, since it has strong connotations of the Roman Catholic tradition from which they broke away.

The funeral service provides an occasion for family and friends to express grief and to acknowledge death's reality and finality. More positively, however, a funeral celebrates the life of the deceased, and is a reminder of the hope of resurrection that Christianity affords. Jesus' words, 'I am the resurrection and the life' (John 11:25), usually feature prominently in the funeral service, which typically consists of prayers, hymns, reading from scripture, and a homily or a tribute to the deceased. Frequently, there are two services: one in church and a second at the graveside or crematorium. In the Roman Catholic and Protestant traditions there is no preference between burial and cremation, but Orthodox Christians insist on burial.

The practice of holding wakes is found in Catholicism and Orthodoxy, but is not favoured by Protestants. It involves ensuring that the deceased is physically accompanied by friends and relatives throughout the period between death and burial. The custom may or may not have its origins in pre-Christian belief that demons might enter the body, as is sometimes speculated. Such a belief certainly plays no part in Christian thinking today. The practice may have the pragmatic function of ensuring that a corpse is not desecrated, but the principal concern is to ensure that the deceased is the constant object of prayer.

Death and Resurrection

What happens after death? The Bible and the Christian creeds affirm the 'resurrection of the body' which is followed by 'the life everlasting'. The majority of Christians believe that death is not the end, but another part of one's journey or pilgrimage. At the time of Jesus, Jewish thought did not conceive of a person as a mind and a body, which were separated at death, but rather as a unity. Many Jews did not appear to believe in any resurrection – the belief may have entered Jewish thought through contact with the Persians. The Bible records that the Sadducees of Jesus' time denied that there was any life after death (Matthew 22:23). As early Christianity came into contact with Greek thought, it tended to absorb its philosophy of viewing the self as essentially a soul or a mind, with the body as a garment that wore out in the course of one's lifetime. This view of the self later gained further momentum through more modern Western philosophers such as René Descartes (1596–1650), who argued that Reason is the essential characteristic of the self ('I think, therefore I am'), and that the soul (one's rational part) is eternal, leaving the body behind on death.

In a passage familiar to many Christians, Paul writes about the resurrection, claiming that what is resurrected is a 'spiritual body' not a 'natural body' (1 Corinthians 15:42–4), suggesting that there will be some kind of transforming of the former into the latter at the resurrection. Paul also affirms that at his resurrection Christ is 'the firstfruits of those who have fallen asleep' (1 Corinthians 15:20). The nature of Jesus' resurrection is therefore supposed to tell the Christian something about the general resurrection that awaits them. The Gospel writers affirm that Jesus' tomb was empty, which suggests a physical resurrection. Other details of resurrection stories seem to confirm this. For example, Jesus meets the disciples at the Sea of Galilee and eats breakfast with them (John 21:1–14); he shows his crucifixion wounds to the disciples and invites Thomas, the doubting disciple, to feel them (John 20:24–9). On the other hand, Mark recounts that he appeared to two disciples 'in a different form' (Mark 16:12). According to Luke, he makes a sudden appearance, causing the disciples to think they are seeing a ghost (Luke 24:37), and he seems to be able to pass through locked doors to visit the disciples (John 20:19), although on both occasions Jesus offers proof that his body is physical. His body appears to have been taken up into heaven (Acts 1:9), which is certainly uncharacteristic of physical bodies.

The majority of Christians believe that Jesus' resurrection was a bodily one, but there are different opinions about whether Christ being the 'firstfruits' of a more general resurrection necessarily means that their next life will be a physical one. A physical resurrection raises a number of obvious problems. Would there be enough room on the earth for so many generations to occupy it simultaneously? Will bodies still be gendered? What would resurrected people look like? Would those who died old still look old, and would children who died still be children? Augustine claimed to solve such conundrums. In his *City of God* he affirms that resurrection bodies will retain their sex, since both men and women were part of God's original paradise. However, women will no longer bear children, and men will no longer be subject to fleshly lusts. One's ideal height will be the same as Jesus during his earthly adulthood, and everyone will be restored or accelerated to the age of 30 – Jesus' age at the beginning of his ministry. All physical blemishes will be removed, and any lost limbs or organs restored. Where a physical body has been dismembered or scattered, God, being omnipotent, will be able to find and reconstitute its parts. As for victims of cannibals, God will decide which parts belong to the victim and which belong to the (presumably penitent) cannibal! Few present-day Christians would claim to have knowledge of the resurrection life in such detail, although some fundamentalists have commented that the size of the earth will not be a problem, since the Bible predicts that the world's desert areas will become fertile (Isaiah 35:1). These problems continue to be debated among philosophers of religion, inevitably with no agreed outcome. Those who favour the immortality of the soul face other difficulties. If those who survive death have no physical bodies, how would they recognize each other? What would they do all day? If immortal life consists of eternally praising God, as scripture implies, how is this possible without the usual means of using one's voice or writing with one's hands?

Christians are of course familiar with the imagery that is associated with the heavenly New Jerusalem: pearly gates, angels playing harps, vast dimensions, with a crystal river flowing through it, no more night, no sun to give light since God himself has unlimited radiance, and the throne of God and the Lamb (Jesus) prominent in the city. There will be no more sorrow, and nothing impure will defile it (Revelation 21 and 22). Even Christian fundamentalists would acknowledge that the Book of Revelation employs difficult imagery, and that such depictions are at best very approximate indications of the joys of heaven, which the human mind is incapable of grasping on this side of eternity.

The Destiny of the Unrighteous

So far we have discussed the kingdom of heaven – the destiny of those who belong to the true Church. Christianity's view of the fate that awaits the unrighteous remains to be considered. Traditionally, Christians have held that there are two eternal destinies: heaven and hell. The latter is described as a place 'where the worm does not die, and the fire is not quenched' (Mark 9:48), and it has been portrayed as a lake of fire, an inferno in a bottomless pit of sulphur, emitting a dreadful stench, a place of relentless agony, with dungeons and ovens where one's body is tortured by demons, with no possibility of escape. Saint Basil (330–79) interpreted the reference to worms to mean that worms would continually devour one's flesh in hell, and Saint Teresa of Avila (1515–82) claimed to have a vision in which she saw the entrance of hell surrounded by venomous insects.

It is difficult to know how literally some Christians have construed such descriptions. There are certainly many descriptions of 'fire and brimstone' preaching, particularly in the nineteenth century. One such example is Father John Furniss, a Roman Catholic priest who devoted much of his life to children's missions. In 1855 he composed a children's book entitled *The Sight of Hell*, with the aim of enabling children to see the possible fate that might await them if they died in a state of mortal sin. The book contains detailed and lurid descriptions of hell, of which the following is but one example:

> See! It is a pitiful sight. The little child is in this red-hot oven. Hear how it screams to come out! See how it turns and twists itself about in the fire! It beats its head against the roof of the oven. It stamps its little feet on the floor of the oven. You can see on the face of this little child what you can see on the faces of all in hell – despair, desperate and horrible! ... God was very good to this child.
>
> (Furniss, 1855, chapter 28)

God's goodness was shown, apparently, by terminating the little child's existence before adulthood, since he or she would have gone on to commit even greater sins, meriting even more severe punishment.

Though I myself once heard a sermon about hell, describing demons with pitchforks tormenting the damned (I am not sure how serious the preacher was), this literalistic view of hell tends to be held only by the more extreme Christian fundamentalists. As with the descriptions of heaven, those who believe in eternal damnation agree that such descriptions are symbolic, and that sinners need not expect literally to be burned in a lake of fire. The state of hell refers to eternal separation from God, since the Bible teaches that God's presence cannot abide sin (Habakkuk 1:13). In contrast with the joys of heaven, separation from God would be a dreadful fate indeed, and such metaphorical descriptions serve to highlight this. Another evangelical preacher on hell, whom I heard as an adolescent, agreed that it was not literal fire and brimstone, but 'something very terrible'.

Whether or not it is possible to give a clear account of what hell is, Christians have traditionally believed that there will be a final judgement, at which Jesus, sitting at God's right hand, will judge the living and the dead, after his return in glory. While many Christians have regarded the fate of the unrighteous as everlasting punishment, others – particularly in the Adventist tradition – have held that their destiny is eternal death, not torment. As the Seventh-day Adventists point out, the Bible states that the wages of sin is death (Romans 6:23), not eternal punishment. Further, the references to the destruction of the wicked mean a 'second death', from which there is no further resurrection: it is annihilation. This was a view supported by no less a figure than Archbishop William Temple in his *Christian Faith and Life* (1931, p. 81). The references to fire mean only that the destruction of the wicked will be complete, just as a fire burns until it has consumed everything that is combustible.

The Bible speaks of two afterlife states apart from heaven, not one: Hades and hell. These are not equivalent, and the Book of Revelation clearly distinguishes them:

> The sea gave up the dead that were in it, and death and Hades gave up the dead that were in them, and each person was judged according to what he had done. Then death and Hades were thrown into the lake of fire. The lake of fire is the second death. If anyone's name was not found written in the book of life, he was thrown into the lake of fire.
>
> (Revelation 20:13–15)

Hades was an underworld, and the word is the Greek equivalent of the Hebrew *sheol*. The Old Testament has little to say about life after death, implying that at best it is but a shadowy half-existence:

For the living know that they will die,
but the dead know nothing;
they have no further reward,
and even the memory of them is forgotten.

(Ecclesiastes 9:5)

According to Luke's Gospel, Jesus speaks of 'the resurrection of the righteous' (Luke 14:14), which has sometimes been construed to mean that there are two resurrections, not one – the righteous being raised first, before a general resurrection involving the righteous and the unrighteous takes place. Many Christian fundamentalists have taken the Bible to suggest a timetable that incorporates a series of end-time events, such as the 'rapture' (or second coming), the Great Tribulation, Armageddon, the destruction of the earth by fire, the 'white throne judgement' (Revelation 20:11), a first and second resurrection, the binding of Satan, the millennium, the unleashing of the devil, and Christ's everlasting rule. There are variations in the sequence, since the Bible does not identify all these events in one single continuous passage. Other Christians contend that it is inappropriate to seek out a coherent programme of events in this way, arguing that we are in the realms of symbol and metaphor, which are used to describe what can only be grasped in a very partial manner.

Roman Catholic Doctrine: Purgatory and Limbo

According to Roman Catholic teaching, there exist two additional states besides heaven and hell. The believer's ultimate goal is 'the vision and beatitude of God' (*Catechism*, 2548), the ability to see God is all his glory, in a perfected state, in communion with him. Jesus said, 'Blessed are the pure in heart, for they will see God' (Matthew 5:8). With the possible exception of the saints and martyrs, few, if any, believers have attained complete purity on death. Purgatory is therefore an intermediate state, in which those who died in a state of grace, but are not yet wholly pure, can receive purification. In popular speech the term 'purgatory' connotes pain, but the state of purgatory, as understood by Roman Catholics, is not unpleasant, but rather purifying. The doctrine was affirmed at the Council of Florence (1439) and again at the Council of Trent (1547). The Roman Catholic Church claims scriptural support for this teaching: Judas Maccabeus performed an act of atonement for those who had died for their faith, in order to expiate their sin (2 Maccabees 12:46). The books of Maccabees are part of the Apocrypha, however, and hence Protestants do not accept that the doctrine of purgatory and the practice of praying for the dead have scriptural warrant.

Another state that seems to lie between heaven and hell is limbo. The word 'limbo' comes from the Latin *limbus*, meaning a border or an edge, and Roman Catholics have speculated that such a place exists for unbaptized infants, and for those who lived before the time of Christ, and hence had no opportunity to hear the gospel. The Apostles' Creed contains the line, 'He descended into hell'. (Modern translations substitute, 'He descended to the dead.') It has been held in all traditions that, between the time of his crucifixion and resurrection, Jesus went to the underworld of Sheol, and preached to the spirits of the departed (1 Peter 3:18–19). The doctrine is sometimes known as 'the harrowing of hell', and is frequently depicted in Christian art.

The position of unbaptized infants is different from those who lived before Christ. They have come into existence after Christ's harrowing of hell. Being unbaptized, they are not part of the Christian Church, and remain tainted with original sin. On the other hand, a small child or, more especially, a stillborn baby or aborted embryo has not committed any evil deeds, and hence eternal punishment in hell would seem inappropriate. Accordingly, some Roman Catholic theologians suggested the notion of limbo as a place that is inferior to heaven, yet not as unpleasant as hell. Unlike purgatory, limbo is not an intermediate stage in one's spiritual refinement, but an eternal one.

In 2005 the media announced that the Vatican had decided to abandon the notion of limbo. Such reports were inaccurate. The doctrine has existed in the Church from ancient times. Gregory of Nazianzus (c. 329–c. 390) was one of the earliest Church Fathers to affirm it. Saint Augustine opposed it, Saint Thomas Aquinas accepted it, and different views have subsequently been expressed through the ages. In 1905 Pope Pius X declared that 'Children who die without baptism go into limbo, where they do not enjoy God, but they do not suffer either, because having Original Sin, and only that, they do not deserve paradise, but neither hell nor purgatory' (quoted in Christian Classics Ethereal Library, 2008).

Despite this statement having been made by a pope, this is not regarded as infallible teaching, and in 1984, Cardinal Joseph Ratzinger (now Pope Benedict XVI) expressed his dissent, describing it as no more than a 'theological hypothesis'. Pope John Paul II had reservations about the doctrine, and it is not mentioned in the 1994 *Catechism of the Catholic Church*. Instead, the *Catechism* reads:

> As regards *children who have died without Baptism*, the Church can only entrust them to the mercy of God, as she does in her funeral rites for them. Indeed, the great mercy of God who desires that all men should be saved, and Jesus' tenderness toward children which caused him to say: "Let the children come to me, do not hinder them," allow us to hope that there is a way of salvation for children who have died without Baptism. All the more urgent is the Church's call not to prevent little children coming to Christ through the gift of holy Baptism.
>
> (*Catechism*, 1261; italics original)

The Vatican's reported change of position was occasioned by Professor John Haldane of St Andrews University, a consultant to the Vatican's Pontifical Council for Culture, who questioned whether heaven, hell and limbo were to be construed as 'places', and remarked, 'God's powers are such that He can overcome the issue of Original Sin as He chooses, according to special circumstances' (*The Scotsman*, 20 April 2007). The upshot of the discussion was that limbo is not a Catholic dogma, and that different views are allowable.

Where are the Dead?

Has life in heaven and hell already started, or does it await Christ's return? Christians sometimes pose this question, but there is not a clear answer. On the one hand, the Bible speaks of Christ's second coming and a final judgement as if these are future events. On the other hand, Jesus tells a parable about a rich man and a beggar, who die and enter hell and heaven respectively (Luke 16:19–31). From hell, the rich man is able to see Abraham in heaven, and requests him to send Lazarus back to his home to warn his brothers to mend their ways, in order to avoid his fate. This may suggest that affairs in heaven and hell exist simultaneously with events on earth, as St John Cassian (c. 360–435) believed, but maybe one should not read too much into the story's details. Jesus was preaching primarily about showing concern for the poor, not giving a discourse on the topography of the spiritual world. Jesus said to the dying thief, 'Today, you will be with me in paradise' (Luke 23:43), thus suggesting that paradise already existed. Opponents of this view have pointed out that first-century Greek did not use punctuation, and that the verse might equally be rendered: 'I tell you truly today: you will be with me in paradise.'

Those traditions in which it is customary to pray to the saints and to the Virgin Mary seem to suggest that their eternal destiny has already commenced. Roman Catholicism refers to purgatory as a purificatory state 'before' the final judgement (*Catechism*, 1031), and the practice of praying for the dead seems to suggest that they exist in a state where the actions of those on earth are capable of helping them. According to Orthodox teaching, at the moment of death the soul leaves the body and begins a 40-day journey to its spiritual destination. It is accompanied by various spiritual beings to whom it is related – angels and demons – and on the journey passes various 'toll-houses'. At these toll-houses the demons attempt to collect their dues that have accrued from past sins, either dragging the spirit inside, or luring it in by temptation. The angels endeavour to protect the spirit, offering guidance and help, raising it to the heights. The spirit can also be assisted by the actions of those who remain on earth, who can offer prayers and Memorials – acts of remembrance that take place after the Divine Liturgy – which are normally observed on the ensuing Sunday and forty days after the person's death. These beliefs reflect the more general expectation that a soul's destiny can be affected by what happens to it in the afterlife, where the process of *theosis* may continue or be retarded. According to Orthodox teaching, it is possible to gain salvation in this transitional stage, and it is the Church's hope that all may be reunited to God. This is a possibility rather than a necessity, however, since God does not coerce souls to repent. At the final judgement, the soul will then be reunited to the body; it is not, though, one's original physical body, but a glorified resurrection body. Orthodox teaching is clear that a choice is to be made between heaven and hell. However, hell is still a place where God's love continues to be shown: the difference between heaven and hell is that 'the wicked … experience as suffering what the saints experience as joy' (Ware, 1963/1983, p. 266).

Mention has been made of spirits, angels and demons, and it may be asked to what extent these are part of Christian belief. Those in the twentieth-century radical Protestant tradition came to regard angels and demons as belonging to a worldview that was now superseded, and recommended that they be 'demythologized'. However, most of Christendom has believed in such supernatural beings. In patristic thought, angels were arranged into ranks. Essentially this was a means of making sense of the various types of supernatural being alluded to in Hebrew scripture as well as in writings of or attributed to Paul (Ephesians 1:21; Colossians 1:16). Pseudo-Dionysius (an anonymous fifth- or sixth-century theologian) was one of the first to arrange them into nine 'choirs': seraphim, cherubim, thrones, dominions (or dominations), virtues, powers, principalities, archangels, angels. These are the 'choirs of angels' to which the well-known Christmas hymn ('O come, all ye faithful') refers. Some Christians also believe they have a 'guardian angel' – a personal spiritual guide to aid them throughout their lives.

Whether there are such beings as Satan and demons is a matter that divides Christians. Many believe that they are real, and there has been a renewed interest in demons and exorcism, particularly in the wake of the film *The Exorcist*, which was released in 1973. Catholics and Anglicans offer a ministry of exorcism, although this is not widely publicized, and a priest can perform a rite to cast out demons or spirits. Those who offer this service are careful not to confuse possession with psychiatric illness, and would only perform exorcisms when conventional remedies had failed. In Protestant fundamentalist circles the casting out of demons is known as 'deliverance ministry', for which scriptural warrant is claimed. Jesus is reported as casting out demons, and instructing his disciples to do the same (Matthew 10:8). More liberal Christians are sceptical about the existence of such beings, and regard references to them as metaphorical ways of describing the powers of evil.

Christians are normally advised not to meddle with the occult (Leviticus 19:31; Acts 19:18–19). Although Orthodox Christians typically hold that the soul hovers over its former physical abode for the first two days, desiring to return, the dead can only be helped through prayer, Memorials, and the sacraments. (Even praying for the dead is rejected completely by Protestants, however.) Contact with the dead is very firmly discouraged, and Spiritualism is strongly criticized. It should be noted, however, that most Spiritualist churches do not claim any Christian identity.

Time and Eternity

The discussion so far might seem to suggest that after-death states such as heaven, hell, purgatory and limbo are continuations of one's life on earth, in unending time. Christians frequently talk as if this were the case, and indeed the expression 'life *after* death' suggests that these states come after one's life on earth is finished. Some Christians undoubtedly think in such terms, and have offered physicalistic descriptions of God's kingdom. Particularly in the Adventist tradition, it is expected that Christ's followers will live in a renewed earth that has been cleansed by fire. Jesus said that the meek would inherit the earth (Matthew 5:5), and this is taken to mean quite literally that the righteous will live unendingly on the earth, with their capital city, the New Jerusalem, in heaven. Human activities will continue: there will be houses, which people will build (Isaiah 65:21), there will be physically restored friends and family, and intellectual and spiritual pursuits – but all at a greatly enhanced level.

Many Christian theologians, however, have declined to accept such a picture, arguing that 'eternal' and 'everlasting' do not mean the same. When Jesus speaks of eternal life, the Greek word used in the New Testament is *aiōnios*, which signifies a higher level of existence, not an infinitely greater quantity of it. Jesus says of his followers, 'I am come that they may have life, and have it to the full' (John 10:10). He also says, 'The time has come. The kingdom of God is near' (Mark 1:15), implying an immediacy concerning the coming of the kingdom. Scholars have labelled this idea 'realized eschatology' – the 'last things' are *now*! God and God's kingdom, on this interpretation of time and eternity, are timeless. A God who is subject to time would be subject to change. God is not a being who is in time, the first of a causal series, but rather a being who lies beyond time. '"I am the Alpha and the Omega," says the Lord God, "who is, and who was, and who is to come, the Almighty"' (Revelation 1:8). When the psalmist writes, 'My times are in your hands' (Psalm 31:15), he arguably perceives God as controlling temporal events from the standpoint of eternity.

God, however, acts in time, becoming a being in time in the form of Jesus Christ. Eternity crosses time at the Incarnation. It does so also at the resurrection: Paul writes that 'the perishable must clothe itself with the imperishable' (1 Corinthians 15:53). The sacrament of Holy Communion is, as noted earlier, a symbol of the divine reaching down to humanity, offering a foretaste in time of the timeless celestial banquet. Mystics too have claimed to have gained sight of the eternal in visions or mystical experiences, and sometimes report that time appeared to stand still. If all this seems to make little sense, the majority of Christians would claim that they cannot fully understand the nature of eternity while they are still within time. As the philosopher Immanuel Kant contended, space and time are categories through which we are compelled to look at the world, and it is difficult to see how things could be any different.

Chapter 9

The Future

Writing about Christianity's past and present is difficult enough, but at least, in doing so, we have evidence to go on. Speculating about its future is harder. Who knows what major events might change the course of world history – political events, natural disasters, wars, and intellectual movements – with a resulting impact on religion? Materialism might tempt people away from religion, continuing the trend of 'secularization' in Europe. On the other hand, revivalist movements can appear unexpectedly and give faith a new lease of life. One can only remark on Christianity's possible futures, identifying a number of pressing issues that appear to need some kind of resolution, and dilemmas that Christianity may face.

Some conservative evangelical Christians, however, mainly in the Protestant tradition, believe they can give confident predictions about the future of the world: the end of the present order is near, they declare, and Armageddon is just around the corner. The disasters we are experiencing on earth – wars, earthquakes, famines and other natural disasters, breakdown in human relationships, false prophets and messiahs, persecution for one's faith – are all phenomena that Jesus predicted as signs of the end of this age (Mark 13). All these are harbingers of Christ's return, which can be expected soon. He will return on the clouds of heaven, visible to all, and the battle of Armageddon will commence – a cosmic conflict between Christ and his angels and Satan and his hosts. Christ will be victorious, and the devil will be consigned to an abyss for a thousand years, after which he will be released and allowed for a short time to continue his work, deceiving the world. He will then attempt to gather the nations together to wage war against Christ, but fire will come down from heaven and consume him, and he will be thrown into a lake of fiery sulphur, where he will be tormented for the rest of eternity.

Parts of the Bible employ apocalyptic imagery of this kind, and a number of phenomena are associated with the end times by Christian fundamentalists. The harbingers of the end consist of a world in chaos: natural disasters, laws of nature being suspended or reversed (the sun becoming dark, and the moon turning to blood); there will be a breakdown of human relationships, in the family and in society: persecution and false teaching, children rebelling against their parents and betraying them. The sequence of events that follows is not wholly apparent. Jesus speaks of the Son of Man returning in the clouds of heaven, breaking into human history and winding up earthly affairs (Mark 13:26), yet elsewhere Jesus, and also Paul, use the metaphor of a thief coming in the night to describe the Son of Man's return (Matthew 24:43; 1 Thessalonians 5:2). Some Christian apocalyptists have resorted to harmonization to resolve the contradiction, concluding that the Bible postulates two end-time phenomena: a silent happening when Christ will discreetly gather his followers up to heaven, and a cosmic occurrence in which he will dramatically return on the clouds.

Other end-time events that the Bible describes include the end of the Gentile times, the appearance of the Two Witnesses, a dragon being cast down to earth, the rise of the Antichrist, the mark of the beast, seven plagues, the fall of Babylon, the 'four horsemen of the apocalypse', the Great Tribulation, the Battle of Armageddon, the binding of Satan, the millennium, the Last Judgement, Christ's 'glorious appearing', the establishment of the new heaven and earth, the sealing of the 144,000, the marriage of the Lamb, and the eternal bliss of the redeemed. However, these events are not listed in the Bible in a single continuous timetable. Some parts of the Bible are distinctively apocalyptic in genre, notably the Book of Revelation, the second half of Daniel, Mark 13 and its parallels in Matthew 24:1–43 and Luke 21:5–36. Other verses, such as Paul's mention of Christ's second coming, plainly refer to end times, while interpreting other biblical passages as end-time predictions is much more speculative. The interpretation of apocalyptic ideas is fraught with problems. Do such passages refer to events anticipating or following Christ's return? Do they describe affairs in heaven or on earth, or both? To what extent is the imagery symbolic, or is it to be taken literally? Do apparent inconsistencies mean we should expect two separate events (as in the case of the secret and public return of Christ)? In what order should we expect them to happen? Some apocalyptists have added other events to the above list. Many Adventists expect a final burning of the earth, in fulfilment of Revelation 18:9, although there is disagreement about whether the earth's burning means its destruction or its purification (since fire can be used for both). A further source of controversy is the role of present-day political events. Some Christian fundamentalists have seen the setting up the state of Israel in 1948 and the subsequent conflicts between Arab and Jew as significant signs of the end, while others are not so sure. In the light of all these problems, it is not surprising that different sets of Christian apocalyptists have reached different conclusions about the pattern of end-time affairs.

One popular attempt to make sense of the apocalyptic calendar is a series of novels by Tim LaHaye and Jerry B. Jenkins. These proved immensely popular, causing televangelist Jerry Falwell to say of the first of these, 'In terms of its impact on Christianity, it's probably greater than that of any other book in modern times, outside the Bible' (*Time Magazine*, 7 February 2005). The first title, *Left Behind*, was published in 1997, and begins in an aircraft in which passengers mysteriously go missing, leaving only their clothes and luggage behind. It transpires that the rapture has taken place, and that the missing people, of whom there are many more on earth, have been caught up into heaven by Christ. The pilot, Captain Rayford Steele, discovers on return that his wife has been 'raptured', but his daughter remains on earth. They and others, who have been loosely associated with their local church, now see the error of their ways and, with the help of their pastor (who is also left behind), form a new spiritual community with the task of surviving the Great Tribulation. Their study of the Bible reveals the end-time events that can be expected, beginning with the 'Wrath of the Lamb' earthquake, which devastates their home city, Chicago. Meanwhile, a journalist who is on Steele's flight has been assigned the task of reporting on a Romanian politician called Nicolae Carpathia, who is rising to power. Carpathia turns out to be the Antichrist of the last times, and becomes the world's ruler.

Remarkably, the Internet continues to operate throughout the many global calamities and enables the Tribulation Force to communicate and disseminate edifying Christian teachings. The ensuing events include the appearance of the Two Witnesses (Revelation 11), who prophesy at Jerusalem's 'Wailing Wall', the assassination and resurrection of the Antichrist, and his imposition of the 'mark of the beast', which everyone is required to display in order to engage in commercial transactions (Revelation 13:17). The Jerusalem Temple is desecrated, but one million believers (the Remnant) escape to Petra, where they receive miraculous divine protection. Armageddon ensues, and is followed by Christ's 'glorious appearing' and the commencement of his millennial rule. The events preceding Armageddon are interspersed with seven 'bowl judgements' – so called because angels pour out a series of appalling plagues on the earth from seven bowls (Revelation 16).

Other authors have explored the end-time genre, exploring the idea of how the world will fare when Christ has claimed his chosen ones. Although it is fiction, there are many conservative Christians, particularly in the United States and Britain, who believe that something like these events can be expected to follow the rapture. Although those who are left behind still have an opportunity to repent and mend their ways, they will have to endure the Great Tribulation, which those who have been raptured will escape.

Scholars of religion tend to assume that prophecies regarding the future will fail. Leon Festinger's study *When Prophecy Fails* (1956) has tended to serve as a model of how some religious groups predict the future, and how they come to terms with the 'cognitive dissonance' that is generated when their predictions fail to materialize. Festinger's study, however, although much cited, was of a small flying saucer group who set definite dates on events that they described with some precision. This differs from Christianity's apocalyptic predictions, which are rarely given definite dates, and which are enshrined in symbolism that makes recognition difficult. Occasionally, small groups of Christians have set dates for precise events: for example, the Adventist William Miller, who expected a dramatic return of Christ in 1843, and subsequently 1844, the non-occurrence of which became known as the Great Disappointment. Christians have expressed an expectation of the 'last things' since the first century, and have been undeterred by the delayed fulfilment of their expectations. Those who believe that apocalyptic literature is predictive have invariably applied the predictions to their own age, not to some previous or subsequent generation, and if their expectations are not fulfilled in the twenty-first century, Christians of new generations will continue to expect an imminent end to the present world order.

The 'Post-Christian' Era?

If the world is not going to end, will Christianity end? There are those who predict that Christianity, or even religion as a whole, will die out, and the term 'post-Christian' has even been used to describe the present era. The view that we are living in a post-Christian age is based on various hypotheses. There is the scientistic view that, just as religion is often believed to have superseded belief in magic, so belief in science will supersede belief in religion.

The theory has been held by different scholars for different reasons. One of the first philosophers to advance the theory of the supersession of science was Auguste Comte (1798–1857), whose ideas were influenced by the evolutionist atmosphere of his time. Comte predicted three broad evolutionary steps relating to religion. Religious belief in personalized deities to whom one prayed and offered devotion would give way to metaphysical belief – that is, men and women would continue to believe in a world that transcended the physical realm, but would not regard themselves as having to pray to its inhabitants or offer devotion. As human knowledge – particularly scientific knowledge – advanced, then human beings would abandon all belief in the supernatural, and rely on scientists. Comte himself devised a scientific substitute for religion, in which the anniversaries of famous scientists were celebrated.

Other predictions that Christianity – as well as religion in general – has no future are to be found in the work of Sigmund Freud (1856–1939) and Karl Marx (1818–83). Freud's attack on religion is found in his *Totem and Taboo* (1913) and *The Future of an Illusion* (1927). He contended that religion was mere wish fulfilment, and that religious rituals were forms of neuroses – obsessive acts, resulting from attempts to control an Oedipus complex. In *Totem and Taboo* Freud suggests that embedded in the believer's subconscious is a myth of the murder of a primal father. This myth resurfaces as a totem, a sacred object or objects surrounded by taboos. Religion, and especially Christianity, alludes to such a myth in its doctrine of original sin, and its quest for redemption by a saviour figure who can remove this guilt.

Karl Marx is renowned for his famous statement that 'religion is the opium of the people'. Marx viewed religion as a tool of the oppressor, who uses it to offer other-worldly hope to the oppressed, thus making them more reconciled to the injustices they experience on earth – a thesis that underlies the communist ideology, which stemmed from his writings. Religion, Marx argued, is inherently irrational; it devalues human dignity by placing the believer in a servile position; and it is hypocritical. Jesus taught compassion and deliverance for the poor, yet the Church has amassed large quantities of wealth for itself. Even Martin Luther, who challenged the wealth of the Catholic Church, nonetheless sided with the rulers against the peasants.

What are we to make of Freud and Marx's prognosis concerning Christianity's future? They accused Christian believers of wishful thinking and hypocrisy, but few people seem to have left the Church specifically on this account. Furthermore, although both posited a dichotomy between science and religion – contending that with the advancement of science, men and women would be drawn to rational ways of understanding the world and that scientific rationality would supersede religious illusion – as we noted in a previous chapter, many scientists continue to feel drawn to religion, and indeed hold that the discoveries of modern science help to shed light on, rather than to detract from, the teachings of the Christian faith.

It is true, as the sociologist Émile Durkheim (1858–1917) later argued, that the Church has had a legitimating function, often sanctioning the affairs of the state. However, it is not the case that political systems such as communism succeeded in abolishing religion in order to remove its supposedly palliative function. It is simply untrue that the period of communist rule in Eastern Europe during the four decades before its demise in 1989 resulted in the disappearance of Christianity in communist states, creating a 'spiritual hunger' that was satisfied by the possibility of a return to religion in the early 1990s. This is a popular, but false idea, to which some evangelical Protestants (as well as some new religious movements) have subscribed, believing that Eastern European countries were ripe for evangelism. Although the churches experienced restrictions under communist regimes, the Catholic and Orthodox Churches survived during that time, with the faithful continuing to attend worship and practise their faith.

Secularization

A more serious threat to Christianity, at least in the West, is the phenomenon of secularization. Secularization means more than simply a decline in church attendance, although this has dwindled considerably in the United Kingdom. In a survey carried out in 2007, 8 per cent of respondents stated that they attended church weekly, and 15 per cent claimed to attend church once a month. This is less than the 20 per cent recorded in 1960 (Tear Fund, 2007; Bruce, 1995, p. 40) and a substantial drop from the (approximately) 50 per cent who attended on the Victorian Census Sunday in 1851. While the significance of such statistics can be debated, there is little doubt that Britain is experiencing a downward trend in church attendance and membership, to the extent that some commentators have suggested that Christianity will be a minority religion by 2050, having been overtaken by Islam, and possibly Hinduism (Gledhill, 2008). The decline is largely caused by ageing congregations, whose numbers are not being replenished to an equal level by a younger generation. With declining congregations comes declining money in the offering bowl, and less income to support church buildings and the salaries of Christianity's religious professionals. According to this prognosis, attendance in the Church of England could decline to 350,000 in the year 2030, restricted to only 10,000 churches, with an average congregation of 35 apiece. By 2050, the Church of England could expect only 87,800 worshippers each Sunday countrywide.

Allied to declining church attendance is the phenomenon of secularization. This is the process whereby erstwhile religious believers do not necessarily espouse some secular alternative to religion, but where the influence of religion upon society becomes diminished, and religion loses its hold on people. Originally the term 'secularization' was applied to the transfer of land from ecclesiastical to secular state ownership, and subsequently in Roman Catholicism, whereby priests could be discharged from a religious order in order to serve society more widely. One notable expression of the secularization thesis is Bryan Wilson's *Religion in Secular Society* (1966). Wilson identifies a number of societal factors which, he believes, have caused a decline in the Church's influence. There has been a decline in the community, due largely to urbanization and social mobility. There is the rise of science and technology. Although Wilson agrees that in reality there is little head-on conflict between science and religion, he argues that this can appear to be so. Technology also provides solutions to problems for which religion was previously invoked: medical treatment in place of prayer, counselling in place of confession and absolution. Although church attendance in the USA remains much higher than Britain's estimated 10 per cent each Sunday, the secularization thesis is held to apply to America as well as Britain: the constituents of secularization still exist, and the churches, although reasonably well attended, arguably exercise less control over people's lives.

It is always difficult to know the extent to which one can rely on projections of past and present statistical trends. Understandably, the Church of England has disputed this analysis of future trends, claiming that the statistics give only a partial view. Some 1.7 million people, the Church of England's research unit has contended, worship in a church or cathedral at least once a month, and this level of allegiance has remained constant from 2000 to 2008. Religious allegiance is a multifaceted phenomenon, and statistical information about weekly attendances is only part of the story. Some churches report increased attendance at midweek services, or seek to create a network of supporters who do not necessarily attend on Sundays. Christianity also reaches out through the media – radio, television and, most recently the Internet, where Christian cyber-communities 'meet' as prayer groups or as online worshippers. The Internet is too recent a phenomenon for us to be able to assess with any accuracy the extent to which Christian online communities overlap traditional 'embodied' church groups or whether they offer a genuine and meaningful alternative to traditional Christian congregations.

Could Christianity be overtaken by some other religion, such as Islam? It has sometimes been suggested that Islam is the fastest growing religion in the world, and that there will be more Muslims than Christians by the year 2050. The concept of the 'fastest growing religion' is fraught with problems (Chryssides and Geaves, 2007, pp. 299–304). Much depends on what is being measured, the periods on which one bases one's measurement, and what 'growth' means: 'growth', for example, can mean total numbers, percentage growth over a given period, or proportion of the 'market share'. On present evidence, Christianity is increasing more rapidly than Islam in terms of total numbers (2 billion in 2000 to a projected total of 2.62 billion in 2025 for Christianity, compared with 1.19 billion in 2000 to a projected 1.78 billion for Islam), but Islam's growth, expressed as a percentage of its adherents in 2000, is higher than Christianity's (150 per cent from 2000 to 2025, compared with 130 per cent). In terms of the 'market share', assuming present trends continue, Christianity would remain at 33 per cent of the world's population, with Islam increasing its share from 20 per cent to 23 per cent, taking most of its share from other world religions, of which percentage adherence would drop from 47 per cent to 44 per cent. This percentage 'drop' is actually an increase in terms of total numbers, since the world's population is increasing (Barrett, 2001, p. 4).

World statistics	2000 (in billions)	2025 (in billions)	Increase (in billions)	Percentage increase	'Market percentage share' 2000	'Market percentage share' 2025

Total Christians	2.00	2.617	0.617	30	33	33
Total Muslims	1.188	1.785	0.597	50	20	23
World population	6.055	7.824	1.769	29	100	100

All this assumes that present trends continue, of course, which they may not.

Christianity's growth is not evenly spread throughout the globe. Growth is considerably more rapid in Africa, Latin America and Asia. In 1900, only 9 per cent of Africa's population were Christian, compared with 46 per cent in 2002. The form of Christianity that emerges in these countries tends to be conservative, interpreting the Bible and creeds in a literal way, with an emphasis on spiritual healing, casting out of demons, apocalyptic expectations, and conservative views on morality, evidenced for example by disapproval of homosexuality. The last of these already causes tensions within Christianity, with Anglicans fearing there could be a split within the Anglican Communion, given that openly gay clergy are being ordained in the West and serious consideration is being given to the blessing of gay partnerships.

One writer – Philip Jenkins (2002) – has speculated that the growth of Christianity in Africa, where he believes that more than half the population will be Christian by 2050, may have implications for political ideologies. Some African countries may not separate Church and state, and thus we may witness the creation of new Christian states. Further, Jenkins points out that Islam is simultaneously growing in these countries, and that this is likely to create tensions between the two religions, as each experiences 'fiery religious revivals' amidst an ever-increasing population. Jenkins suggests that as different communities vie with each other for resources, physical conflict could break out in the guise of twenty-first-century religious war. This is speculation, however. Certainly, on present showing, conservative and charismatic expressions of Christianity are the versions that are accompanied by missionary activity, with a decline in liberal expressions of the Christian faith. However, just as many Western Christians came to accept less conservative versions of their faith in the nineteenth and twentieth centuries, so the intellectual climate of Africa, Latin America and Asia could change. It is possible, too, that liberal Christians might decide to do more to promote liberal Christianity. As far as conflict over the world's resources is concerned, it is also possible that such problems may be addressed by interreligious cooperation, rather than by conflict, as the interfaith movement progresses on a global scale.

The Future: The Church in the World

The Church's future is about more than its expansion and its developing theology. The Church is set in the midst of the world, and its mission extends beyond its own institutions. The world's concerns are the Church's, and one of the important arms of the World Council of Churches is its Commission of the Churches on International Affairs, which deals with issues such as peace, justice, and care for the planet. Most of the larger Christian denominations incorporate central departments dealing with social responsibility, and are endeavouring to ensure that the earth has a viable future, the ideal being a world where love, peace and justice are truly realized.

One major area of concern is humanity's use of the earth's resources. In 1967 historian Lynn White (1907–87) wrote an article entitled 'The Historical Roots of Our Ecologic Crisis'. Despite being a Christian himself, his argument was that Christianity had largely contributed to the earth's predicament. White identified the Industrial Revolution as the turning point, since modern science and technology created the means for humanity to exploit and even destroy the planet. Christian teaching that humanity has been given dominion over the earth led, he believed, to an anthropocentric view of the world in which human beings see themselves as superior to the rest of creation, and view nature as existing for their own purposes. The pagan religions that were displaced by Christianity emphasized the importance of nature, frequently regarding it as being permeated by spirits. By contrast, Christianity substituted a cult of saints – human beings whose existence is not on earth, but in heaven. White singles out Saint Francis, with his concern for animal life and for the whole of creation, as one exception to Christianity's anthropocentric tendencies, but regrets that the Franciscan ethic is not more widely embraced by Christians.

White's challenge to Christianity's environmental record has elicited both theological and practical responses, and even the most conservative Christian denominations take seriously the need to ensure the earth's continuing survival. Few Christians deny that there are problems of global warming and climate change, although more controversial is the question of the extent to which humankind is responsible for these changes. The fundamentalist Southern Baptists acknowledge the natural order as God's 'cosmic revelation': nature, they believe, offers compelling evidence of God's existence and authorship of the world for those who are unfamiliar with the Bible. Most Christians would now agree that the dominion God is said to have given to Adam at the world's beginning is not to be interpreted as domination and unlimited control of the planet's resources, but rather as stewardship. The theme of stewardship or management of resources is found on a number of occasions in Jesus' teaching, and it is now commonplace for Christians to use the concept in connection with the earth's resources.

Two religious responses have gone further than simply emphasizing stewardship. Eco-feminism views the traditional patriarchal system whereby women have been subjugated as being connected to the masculine tendency to dominate not only women, but the whole of the natural environment, including animals and inanimate resources. There is no single agreed version of eco-feminism. However, many eco-feminists are highly critical of the problems that have resulted in a world in which men typically own the land: deforestation, soil erosion, overgrazing of pastures, pollution, and toxic waste. Many draw attention to female problems, which they believe are attributable to a male-dominated world, such as a marked increase in breast cancer, the use of carcinogens to manufacture cosmetics, and increased levels of mercury in the bloodstream leading to foetal deformities. Eco-feminism is essentially a socio-political movement, but it has spiritual repercussions, viewing the earth as sacred and in need of liberation from male domination. Those who espouse eco-feminism may feel constrained either to move outside Christianity, into goddess spirituality or neo-Paganism, or else to help shape new expressions of the Christian faith that incorporate more distinctively feminine aspects.

The second response is Creation Spirituality. The expression was first used by the German philosopher K. C. F. Krause (1781–1832), but it is now firmly associated with Matthew Fox (b. 1940), whose key work is *Original Blessing: A Primer in Creation Spirituality* (1983). Fox was a Dominican priest, until Cardinal Joseph Ratzinger (now Pope Benedict XVI) expelled him from the order in 1988 for his denial of the doctrine of original sin. He subsequently joined the Episcopal Church of America. Fox's concern is the healing of divisions, between the sacred and the secular, spirituality and social justice, mysticism and prophecy. God is to be seen in all the world (Fox can be said to be a panentheist), and humanity should 'enjoy creation rightly' (Fox, 1983, pp. 124–5). The world is a place to be valued, and the contemplation of God is not to be divorced from the prophetic denunciation of social injustice. Fox advocates a fourfold path: a *via positiva* ('positive way' – joy and delight at God's world), a *via negativa* ('negative way' – silence, letting go, in the face of suffering and evil), a *via creativa* ('creative way' – creativity that incorporates delight and suffering), and a *via transformativa* ('transformative way' – transforming the world into a just, compassionate and interdependent whole). Fox's spirituality thus combines care for the environment with love for God. Fox typically refers to God as 'Mother', emphasizing her role in nature, and in his recent *The Hidden Spirituality of Men* (2008), Fox advocates the need for openness to a more healthy form of masculinity, which he believes is not currently found in the Christian faith.

Care for the environment goes beyond self-preservation. As many Christians have come to realize, the effects of climate change are likely to have a damaging impact on developing countries before the more affluent West experiences its effects. Already the Third World's population is coming to experience the scorching of agricultural land, the drying up of lakes used for irrigation and fishing, and a resultant decrease in the availability of food coupled with an increase in its cost. Climatologists predict an increase in heat waves, storms and periods of drought. Westerners, who arguably have attained their high standards of living through the exploitation of the earth's resources, have created many of the problems the Third World experiences, and the Third World lacks the financial resources to afford more efficient technology. Problems of climate intertwine with issues of economic justice. These problems have no easy solution, and will continue to challenge Christians in the twenty-first century and perhaps beyond.

Stewardship of the environment therefore does not merely call for the continued development of eco-theology. It calls for action, in which Christians are becoming increasingly involved at a number of levels. Christian relief organizations such as Christian Aid and the Catholic Agency for Overseas Development (CAFOD) continue to work at a number of levels. For the average Christian, the easiest and most obvious method of involvement is charitable giving. Many Protestant churches take part in Christian Aid Week, which normally occurs annually in May, to raise funds by congregational and door-to-door collection, as well as organizing fund-raising events. In addition to fund-raising, there is consciousness-raising. Christian relief organizations endeavour to raise awareness, not only at congregational level, but also at societal level. At the time of writing, Christian Aid warns of the problems caused by the West's use of bio-fuels, which divert resources that might otherwise be used for food, causing increased food prices in Central America. It also organized a 'Countdown to Copenhagen' campaign, aimed at influencing political leaders to attend the 2009 UN Copenhagen climate summit, to secure the implementation of appropriate policies on climate change. It goes without saying, of course, that these Christian relief organizations also implement projects in developing countries to combat poverty and injustice. Campaigns for fairly traded goods are now well established and likely to continue. Traidcraft, a Christian charitable organization and trading company, was established in 1979, and pioneered non-exploitative trade with workers in developing countries. Local churches in the UK can apply to become 'Fairtrade churches' by undertaking to serve only fairly traded tea and coffee after worship and at meetings, extending this policy to cover other commodities, and participating in an annual Fairtrade Fortnight. The Fairtrade Foundation was set up in 1992 as a collaborative effort on the part of various Christian organizations, including Christian Aid, CAFOD and the World Development Movement. It has now brought in secular organizations with similar interests, and its work has extended beyond its 4,000 Fairtrade churches, with 37 Jewish synagogues and 60 universities attaining Fairtrade status.

At a local level, many Christians are becoming aware of their environmental responsibilities, and building these into congregational policies. The design and maintenance of churches is increasingly taking into account ecological principles, with new buildings being designed to conserve energy. Planting trees, insulation, the use of daylight to minimize the need for artificial lighting, and the creation of roof gardens are just some of the measures that churches, particularly in the United States and Canada, have employed to reduce their use of the earth's resources. Many churches, particularly in European countries, however, are historic buildings, often large and costly to heat, light and generally maintain. In many instances, congregations are faced with situations where their church building is of architectural interest and therefore cannot legally be demolished or altered at will. Such congregations are understandably concerned about how they manage their future, with rising costs, frequently coupled with dwindling congregations. Equally important is the question of stewardship of financial resources: is it right for a congregation to be obliged to maintain obsolete buildings at the expense of financing the Church's wider mission to the community and beyond?

A number of churches have explored innovatory ways of tackling such problems, and we may see more of these as the twenty-first century progresses. Some older churches have divided their buildings up, recognizing that they no longer need the full area of a traditional church. In the town in which the author resides, one church decided to convert its building into a shopping precinct, with small shops – including a Christian bookshop – at ground level, with a café and a new, smaller, worship area above, which shoppers are invited to use for prayer and reflection. The new configuration not only provides the congregation with revenue, but places the church among the people. Some sacrifices have to be made when such conversions take place: for example, in the case above, the large organ that once provided the music could not be left intact, and the congregation decided to opt for a good piano instead. Other congregations have questioned whether it makes sense for church premises to lie empty for the larger part of the week, and have explored schemes whereby their buildings, sometimes including the sanctuary area, can be rented out for secular purposes. Alternative uses of the sanctuary are problematic, however. Many Christians regard the sanctuary area as holy, and therefore set apart from worldly use. There are also practicalities: although sanctuary areas are under-utilized, they are needed – often unexpectedly – for life-cycle events such as funerals. A further way of rationalizing physical resources is ecumenical cooperation, and there are now many examples in Britain of premises being jointly used by different denominations. As ecumenical relationships progress, and resources continue to be a problem, such arrangements may well become more commonplace.

Christianity's Outstanding Agenda

The twenty-first century undoubtedly presents numerous issues on which there will be continued debate, and which will impact on each other. Christian ecumenism is set to continue, but not with a view to producing one homogeneous Christian Church. Relationships will be affected by tensions between Christianity's conservative and liberal camps, with issues such as biblical literalism, morality and attitudes to homosexuality continuing not only to divide opinion, but to risk splits in religious traditions, particularly Anglicanism. Women's ordination remains a divisive factor: although some denominations now unequivocally accept it, the Anglican tradition is still faced with the question of whether the Forward in Faith movement will die out as ordained women become more commonplace, or whether divisions of opinion will continue to need accommodating. There remains the issue of women bishops, and how that would impact on the ordination of priests and deacons more widely. With the reluctance of Roman Catholicism and Eastern Orthodoxy to accept women's ordination – not to mention the attitudes of the more conservative Protestant denominations – there can be little doubt that this matter will have an important bearing on ecumenism.

As science and technology advance, the Church appears set to work with scientific progress and to use its results. The one substantial area of conflict lies in the creationist–evolutionist controversy, which currently shows no signs of being resolved. In other areas, Christians welcome modern research in physics, biology and medicine, although they are sensitive to their ethical implications. Computing, information technology and the Internet will continue to aid the Church's work, although here too church leaders, such as the Archbishop of Canterbury, have voiced caution about possible dangers, particularly to children, such as the stultifying of personal relationships as people immerse themselves almost wholly in online social networks or exposure to potentially damaging online material. The future development of cyber-churches is uncertain. There has been one notable experiment in this area, sponsored by the Methodist Church, which sought to provide a facility for people to worship from their homes in an interactive way. Many forms of worship – for example, receiving the sacraments – seem to require the sharing of physical space, and it remains to be determined whether new forms of worship can be devised that would not depend on physical proximity. Certainly the Internet will continue to provide an important resource for the churches, particularly in terms of outreach, since it allows them to put across their message in a non-threatening way while permitting outsiders to access this anonymously.

A more controversial problem posed by modern technology relates to the prolongation of life and existence of an increasingly ageing population, particularly in the West, where advances in modern medicine have resulted in people living longer. The phenomenon is already causing tensions: should retirement ages be extended to reduce reliance on pension funds, or should older people retire to create jobs for the younger members of the population? As the world's population increases, placing increasing strain on the earth's resources, might we see a change in those traditions that have been opposed to artificial forms of contraception? Might we see less emphasis on prolonging life when its quality is low but expensive to maintain? Should the churches accept that death is perhaps not the ultimate enemy (1 Corinthians 15:26), and that allowing someone to die, or even actively terminating the life of a terminally ill patient, might ultimately be a more humane and humanitarian act than prolonging it? Without venturing to predict any outcomes of such debate, it seems likely that this is an issue that the churches will be constrained to address.

The topic of death raises questions about expectations beyond death's boundaries. Apart from a handful of more radically inclined Christians who have questioned the notion of an afterlife, Christianity has taught the doctrine of the resurrection, and has an expectation that there is a life to be experienced beyond our present earthly one. Hope is one of the cardinal Christian virtues, although perhaps the least articulated of Paul's trio of 'faith, hope and love' (1 Corinthians 13:13). As we have seen, some conservative Christians, particularly in the Calvinist tradition, fully expect two contrasting destinies – heaven and hell – for the faithful and the damned respectively. Others are less certain about whether a loving God would regard eternal damnation as a fitting punishment, even for the most atrocious crimes. Some Christians, particularly in the Adventist tradition, expect only the resurrection of the righteous, holding that eternal destruction (that is, complete oblivion) awaits the wicked, rather than everlasting agony in the fires of hell. For other Christians, universalism has a greater appeal: perhaps a loving God would ensure that everyone was eventually brought to a state of perfection in God's kingdom. The Roman Catholic idea of purgatory serves as the means of such purification, and this notion has begun to appeal even to some theologians in the Protestant tradition, for example John Hick. Again, those Christians who emphasize a social gospel conceive of the future as 'heaven on earth', a world where there is perfect justice, harmony, peace and love. As Augustine wrote, the Christian life is a pilgrimage on earth, to which Christians do not wholly belong. As members of God's celestial kingdom they are on a journey to a celestial city, whose nature far exceeds any earthly expectations. In the Book of Revelation John describes the final goal thus:

I saw the Holy City, the new Jerusalem, coming down out of heaven from God, prepared as a bride beautifully dressed for her husband. And I heard a loud voice from the throne saying, 'Now the dwelling of God is with men, and he will live with them. They will be his people, and God himself will be with them and be their God. He will wipe every tear from their eyes. There will be no more death or mourning or crying or pain, for the old order of things has passed away.'

(Revelation 21:1–4)

Christians differ as to how to interpret John's vision. How literally should they take it? Will this take place in heaven or on earth? Who will belong to this heavenly 'city'? Will its existence take place in continuing everlasting time, or is eternity a state of timelessness? Few Christians are likely to be dogmatic on such issues, instead acknowledging limits to their understanding. No doubt they would agree with Augustine that the nature and membership of this city are known only to God.

Bibliography

Publications Cited in the Text

Archbishops' Council (2000), *Common Worship: Services and Prayers for the Church of England*, London: Church House Publishing.

Athanasian Creed (n.d.), available online at www.ccel.org/creeds/athanasian.creed. html, accessed 11 April 2008.

Barna, George (2008), 'New Marriage and Divorce Statistics Released', 31 March, http://www.barna.org/barna-update/article/15-familykids/42-new-marriage-and-divorce-statistics-released, accessed 16 October 2009.

Barrett, David A. (2001), 'World Christian Encyclopedia', http://www.bible.ca/global-religion-statistics-world-christian-encyclopedia.htm, accessed 14 September 2009.

Barsham, Dinah *et al.* (1987), *Religion: Conformity and Controversy*, Milton Keynes: Open University Press.

Behe, Michael J. (1996), *Darwin's Black Box*, New York: Free Press.

Benford, M. S. and Marino, J. G. (2008), 'Discrepancies in the Radiocarbon Dating Area of the Turin Shroud', *Chemistry Today*, 26 (4), July/August 2008.

Bowden, John (ed.) (2005), *Christianity: The Complete Guide*, London: Continuum.

Bruce, Steve (1995), *Religion in Modern Britain*, Oxford: Oxford University Press.

Bultmann, Rudolf (1958), *Jesus and the Word*, London and Glasgow: Collins.

Bultmann, Rudolf (1960), *Jesus Christ and Mythology*, London: SCM.

Christian Aid (2009), *Growing Pains: The Possibilities and Problems of Biofuels*, available online at http://www.christianaid.org.uk/images/biofuels-report-09.pdf, accessed 16 October 2009.

Christian Classics Ethereal Library (2008), 'The Book of Life', available online at http://www.ccel.org/node/4646/16906, accessed 16 October 2009.

Chryssides, George D. and Geaves, Ron (2007), *The Study of Religion: An Introduction to Key Ideas and Methods*, London: Continuum.

Church of England (1662/1968), *Book of Common Prayer*, London: Collins.

Commission on Faith and Order (1982), *Baptism, Eucharist and Ministry*, Faith and

Order Paper no. 111, Geneva: World Council of Churches.

Darwin, Charles (1859/1872), *The Origin of Species*, London: Odhams.

Davis, Percival W. and Kenyon, Dean H. (1993), *Of Pandas and People: The Central Question of Biological Origins*, Dallas, TX: Haughton Publishing Company.

Dawkins, Richard (2006), *The God Delusion*, London: Bantam.

Dossey, Larry (2001), 'Prescription for Prayer', *Southern California Physician*, 46, December.

Farquhar, J. N. (1913/1930), *The Crown of Hinduism*, Oxford: Oxford University Press.

Festinger, Leon, Riecken, Henry W. and Schachter, Stanley (1956), *When Prophecy Fails: A Social and Psychological Study of a Modern Group that Predicted the Destruction of the World*, New York: Harper and Row.

Flamm, Bruce L. (2004–5), 'Inherent Dangers of Faith-healing Studies', *Scientific Review of Alternative Medicine*, 8 (2), Fall/Winter; www.sram.org/0802/faith-healing.html.

Fletcher, Joseph (1966), *Situation Ethics: The New Morality*, London: SCM.

Forward in Faith (1994), Code of Practice, available online at http://www.forwardinfaith.com/about/uk_code_of_pract.html, accessed 23 August 2009.

Fox, Matthew (1983), *Original Blessing: A Primer in Creation Spirituality*, Rochester, VT: Bear & Company.

Fox, Matthew (2008), *The Hidden Spirituality of Men*, Novato, CA: New World Library.

Freud, Sigmund (1913), *Totem and Taboo*, London: Kegan Paul, Trench, Trubner.

Freud, Sigmund (1928), *The Future of an Illusion*, London: Hogarth Press.

Furniss, John (1855/1866), *The Sight of Hell*, Dublin: James Duffy, available online at http://home.earthlink.net/~jehdjh/kidlit1.html#doing, accessed 17 August 2009.

Galton, Francis (1872), 'Statistical Enquiries into the Efficacy of Prayer', *The Fortnightly Review*, no. LXVIII, 1 August, pp. 125–35, available online at http://www.abelard.org/galton/galton.htm#prayer, accessed 31 August 2009.

General Conference of Seventh-day Adventists (1989), *Seventh-day Adventists Believe: A Biblical Exposition of 27 Fundamental Doctrines*, Washington, DC: Ministerial Association, General Conference of Seventh-day Adventists.

Gledhill, Ruth (2008), 'Churchgoing on its Knees as Christianity Falls out of Favour', *The Times*, 8 May 2008, available online at http://www.timesonline.co.uk/tol/comment/faith/article3890080.ece, accessed 12 September 2009.

Harris, W. S. *et al.* (1999), 'A Randomized, Controlled Trial of the Effects of Remote, Intercessory Prayer on Outcomes in Patients Admitted to the Coronary Care Unit', *Archives of International Medicine*, 159 (19), pp. 2273–8.

Hick, John and Hebblethwaite, Brian (eds) (1980), *Christianity and Other Religions: Selected Readings*, Glasgow: Fount.

Holy Bible (1978), *New International Version*, London: Hodder & Stoughton.

Hoose, Jayne (ed.) (1999), *Conscience in World Religions*, Leominster, England and Notre Dame, Indianapolis: Gracewing and University of Notre Dame Presses.

Irons, Peter (2007), 'Disaster in Dover: The Trials (and Tribulations) of Intelligent Design', *Montana Law Review*, 68, 2007, pp. 60–87.

Isherwood, L. and McEwan, D. (1996), *An A–Z of Feminist Theology*, Sheffield: Sheffield Academic Press.

Jenkins, Philip (2002), 'The Next Christianity', *Atlantic Monthly*, October, available online at http://www.theatlantic.com/doc/200210/jenkins, accessed 14 September 2009.

LaHaye, Tim and Jenkins, Jerry B. (1995), *Left Behind: A Novel of the Earth's Last Days*, Wheaton, IL: Tyndale House.

Lake, Kirsopp (1907), *The Historical Evidence for the Resurrection of Jesus Christ*, London: Williams and Norgate.

Luther, Martin (1521), 'Against Latomus'; in Teigen (1982), p. 148.

Mack, Burton L. (1993), *The Lost Gospel: The Book of Q and Christian Origins*, Shaftesbury, England: Element.

Marshall, John W. (ed.) (1996–2001), 'The Five Gospel Parallels', University of Toronto, available online at http://www.utoronto.ca/religion/synopsis/meta-5g.htm, accessed 16 October 2009.

Masters, K. S., Spielmans, G. I. and Goodson, J. T. (2006), 'Are There Demonstrable Effects of Distant Intercessory Prayer? A Meta-analytic Review', *Annals of Behavioral Medicine*, 31 (4), pp. 337–42.

McGinty, Stephen (2005), 'Pope to Abandon Idea of Unbaptised Babies Suspended Forever in Limbo', *The Scotsman*, 30 November, available online at http://www. religionnewsblog.com/12945/pope-to-abandon-idea-unbaptised-babies-suspended-forever-in-limbo, accessed 19 August 2009.

Means, John O. (ed.) (1876), *The Prayer-Gauge Debate*, Boston: Congregational Publishing Company, available online at http://ia350605.us.archive.org//load_djvu_ applet.php?file=2/items/prayergaugedeba00meangoog/praycrgaugedeba00meangoog. djvu, accessed 31 August 2009.

Online Christian Library of Virtual Theological Resources (2009), 'Later Creeds', http://www.ntslibrary.com/PDF%20Books/LATER%20CREEDS.pdf, accessed 4 August 2009.

Peacocke, Arthur (2004), *Evolution: The Disguised Friend of Faith?*, Philadelphia and London: Templeton Foundation Press.

Pew Forum on Religion and Public Life / U.S. Religious Landscape Survey (2007), http://religions.pewforum.org/pdf/report2religious-landscape-study-chapter-1.pdf, accessed 30 August 2009.

Pope Paul VI (1965), *Gaudium et Spes* ('Joy and Hope'), available online at http://www. vatican.va/archive/hist_councils/ii_vatican_council/documents/vat-ii_ cons_19651207_gaudium-et-spes_en.htmla, accessed 16 October 2009.

Pope John Paul II (1994), Apostolic Letter *Ordinatio Sacerdotalis* of John Paul II to the Bishops of the Catholic Church on Reserving Priestly Ordination to Men Alone, available online at http://www.vatican.va/holy_father/john_paul_ii/apost_letters/documents/hf_jp-ii_apl_22051994_ordinatio-sacerdotalis_en.html, accessed 23 August 2009.

Powell, Mark Allan (1998), *The Jesus Debate: Modern Historians Investigate the Life of Christ*, Oxford: Lion.

Ratzinger, Joseph (Pope Benedict XVI) (2007), *Jesus of Nazareth*, London: Bloomsbury.

Regnerus, Mark (2009), 'The Case for Early Marriage', *Christianity Today*, 31 July, available online at http://www.christianitytoday.com/ct/2009/august/16.22.html, accessed 5 October 2009.

Robinson, Bruce A. (2005), 'Women's Ordination: The Continuing Debate', Ontario Consultants on Religious Tolerance, available online at http://www.religioustolerance.org/femclrg7.htm, accessed 23 August 2009.

Robinson, J. A. T. (1963), *Honest to God*, London: SCM.

Rogers, Raymond N. (2005), 'Studies on the Radiocarbon Sample from the Shroud of Turin', *Thermochimica Acta*, 425 (1–2), pp. 89–194.

Schweitzer, Albert (1910/1963), *The Quest of the Historical Jesus*, London: Adam and Charles Black.

Scofield, C. I. (1909/1945), *The Scofield Reference Bible*, New York: Oxford University Press.

Smith, Morton (1978), *Jesus the Magician*, London: Gollancz.

Tearfund (2007), *Churchgoing in the UK*, Teddington, Middlesex: Tearfund.

Teigen, Erling T. (1982), 'The Clarity of Scripture and Hermeneutical Principles in the Lutheran Confessions', *Concordia Theological Quarterly*, 46 (2–3), April–July, available online at http://www.ctsfw.edu/library/files/pb/1569, accessed 4 August 2009.

Temple, William (1931) *Christian Faith and Life*, New York: Macmillan.

Tyndall, John (1874), 'Address by President of the Mathematics and Physics Section', *British Association for the Advancement of Science*, pp. lxvi–xcvii.

Vatican (1965), *Nostra Aetate* ('In Our Age'), Vatican City: Libreria Editrice Vaticana.

Vatican (1994), *Catechism of the Catholic Church*, London: Geoffrey Chapman.

Vermes, Geza (1973), *Jesus the Jew: A Historian's Reading of the Gospels*, London: Collins.

Ware, Timothy (1963/1983), *The Orthodox Church*, Harmondsworth: Penguin.

Westminster Confession of Faith (1647/1969), Edinburgh: William Blackwood and Sons.

White, Lynn (1967), 'The Historical Roots of our Ecologic Crisis', *Science*, 155 (3767), March, pp. 1203–7, available online at http://www.rci.rutgers.edu/~hallman/PDF/Roots.pdf, accessed 15 September 2009.

Wilson, Bryan (1966) *Religion in Secular Society*, Harmondsworth: Penguin.

World Council of Churches (1983), *Baptism, Eucharist and Ministry*, Geneva: World Council of Churches.

World Council of Churches, Constitution and Rules of the World Council of Churches, (as amended by the 9th Assembly, Porto Alegre, Brazil, February 2006), available online at http://www.oikoumene.org/en/resources/documents/assembly/porto-alegre-2006/1-statements-documents-adopted/institutional-issues/constitution-and-rules-as-adopted.html, accessed 4 August 2009.

Wright, N. T. (1991), 'How Can the Bible be Authoritative?' (The Laing Lecture 1989, and the Griffith Thomas Lecture 1989), originally published in *Vox Evangelica*, 21, 1991, pp. 7–32, available online at http://www.ntwrightpage.com/Wright_Bible_Authoritative.htm, accessed 3 August 2009.

For further reading

Chryssides, George D. and Wilkins, Margaret Z. (2010), *Christians in the Twenty-first Century*, London: Equinox.

Dowley, T. (1996), *The History of Christianity* (A Lion Handbook), Oxford: Lion.

Hale, Rosemary Drage (2004), *Understanding Christianity*, London: Duncan Baird.

Lindberg, Carter (2006), *A Brief History of Christianity*, Oxford: Blackwell.

Taylor, Richard (2003), *How to Read a Church*, London: Rider.

Woodhead, Linda (2004), *Christianity: A Very Short Introduction*, Oxford: Oxford University Press.

Index